ROUGH GUIDES

POCKET **ROUGH GUIDE**
FLORENCE

this fifth edition updated by
ANNIE WARREN

CONTENTS

FLORENCE

If one city could be said to encapsulate the true essence of Italy it might well be Florence (Firenze in Italian), the first city to be named capital when Italy was unified in 1861. Today's modern Italian language evolved from Tuscan dialect, and Dante's Divina Commedia was the first great work of Italian literature to be written in the vernacular; but what makes this city pivotal to the culture not just of Italy but of all Europe is the Renaissance. The very name by which we refer to this extraordinary era was coined by a Tuscan, Giorgio Vasari, who wrote in the sixteenth century of the "rebirth" of the arts with the humanism of Giotto and his successors. Every eminent artistic figure from Giotto onwards – Masaccio, Donatello, Botticelli, Leonardo da Vinci, Michelangelo – is represented well in Florence in an unrivalled concentration of churches, galleries and museums.

Fountain of Neptune in Piazza della Signoria

During the fifteenth century, architects such as Brunelleschi and Alberti began to transform the cityscape of Florence, raising buildings that were to provide future generations with examples from which to take a lead. As soon as you step out of the train station the imprint of the Renaissance is visible, with the pinnacle of Brunelleschi's stupendous dome visible over the rooftops, and the Renaissance emphasis on harmony is exemplified with unrivalled eloquence in Brunelleschi's interiors of **San Lorenzo**, **Santo Spirito** and the **Cappella dei Pazzi**, and in Alberti's work at Santa Maria Novella and the Palazzo Rucellai. In painting, the development of the new sensibility can be plotted stage by stage in the vast picture collection of the **Uffizi**, while the **Bargello**, the **Museo dell'Opera del Duomo** and the mighty guild church of **Orsanmichele** do the same for the story of sculpture. Equally revelatory are the fabulously decorated chapels of **Santa Croce** and **Santa Maria Novella**, forerunners of such astonishing creations as Masaccio's frescoes at **Santa Maria del Carmine**, Fra' Angelico's serene paintings at **San Marco**, and Andrea del Sarto's work at **Santissima Annunziata**, to name just a few. Florence is the city of Michelangelo, one of the dominant creative figures of sixteenth-century Italy, the scope of whose genius can only be appreciated after you've seen his astonishing San Lorenzo's **Sagrestia Nuova** and the marble statuary of the **Accademia** – home of the *David*. Michelangelo's two great rivals, Raphael and Titian, along with dozens of other supreme painters, are on show in the enormous art gallery of the **Palazzo Pitti,** once the home of the city's most famous family, the Medici, whose former home – the beautiful **Palazzo Medici-Riccardi** – can also be visited.

The achievements of the Renaissance were of course underpinned by the wealth that had been accumulated in earlier decades by the Medici and Florence's other plutocratic dynasties, and in every quarter of the centre you'll see churches and monuments that attest to the financial might of medieval Florence: the Duomo, the Baptistery, the Palazzo Vecchio, the huge churches of Santa Croce and Santa Maria Novella, and the exquisite Romanesque gem of San Miniato al Monte are among the most conspicuous demonstrations

What's new

For tourists, the most significant change in Florence in recent years has been the reopening of the Uffizi in 2021 after various periods of closure due to renovations and the Covid-19 pandemic. The bulk of the work happened on the first floor, which now boasts new rooms and over two hundred additional artworks as the museum makes an effort to display more art by underrepresented groups such as women and people of colour. On leaving the gallery, you'll find another of Florence's significant reopenings; the Florence branch of department store Coin set up shop in a new location at the end of 2022, a refurbished seventeenth-century building near to the exit of the Uffizi. Also relatively recently (in Florentine terms, at least) was the spectacular rebuilding of the Museo dell'Opera del Duomo in 2015 and the transformation of the city's main market, the Mercato Centrale, which now houses a host of late-opening places to eat and drink.

The Last Supper by Domenico Ghirlandaio, Museo di San Marco

of Florence's prosperity. As for the centuries that followed the heyday of the Renaissance, it's often forgotten that Florence played a major role in the development of modern science – this was, after all, the home of **Galileo**, whose name has been bestowed on the city's fascinating science museum.

It can often seem that Florence has become too popular for its own good, a victim of its own success. The city has been a magnet for tourists since the nineteenth century, when Stendhal staggered around its streets in a stupor of aesthetic delight, and nowadays, in high season, parts of the city can be almost unbearably busy, with immense queues for the Uffizi and pedestrian traffic at a standstill on the Ponte Vecchio. But if you time your visit carefully, don't rush around trying to see everything and make a point of eating and drinking in our recommended restaurants, cafés and bars, you'll have a visit you'll never forget.

When to visit

Midsummer in Florence can be unpleasant: the heat is often stifling, and the inundation of tourists makes the major attractions a purgatorial experience. For the most enjoyable visit, arrive shortly before **Easter** or in **October**: the weather should be fine, and the balance between Florentines and outsiders at a more manageable level. Winter can be quite rainy, but the absence of crowds makes the off season a great option for the big sights, many of which are indoors. If you can only travel between Easter and September, be sure to reserve your accommodation well before you arrive, as it's not uncommon for every hotel in the centre to be fully booked. It's not advised to visit Florence (or indeed any major Italian city) in **August**, as this is when the heat becomes too much to bear and the majority of Italians take their holidays, with the result that many restaurants and bars are closed for the entire month.

Where to...

Shop

Florence is known as a producer of **luxury items**, notably gold
jewellery, high-quality leather goods, top-grade stationery and
marbled paper. The whole Ponte Vecchio is crammed with
goldsmiths, but the city's premier shopping thoroughfare is **Via de'
Tornabuoni**, where you'll find the showrooms of Italy's top fashion
designers. Prada, Gucci, Armani, Dolce & Gabbana are all here, as
are the country's main outlets for three of the top Florentine fashion
houses – Pucci, Roberto Cavalli and Ferragamo. For cheap and
cheerful stuff there's the plethora of stalls around San Lorenzo, and
there's also a handful of good **department stores**.
OUR FAVOURITES: Aquaflor, see page 88; Barberino Designer Outlet, see page
112; Giulio Giannini e Figlio, see page 104.

Eat

As you'd expect in a major tourist city, Florence has plenty of
restaurants, but – unsurprisingly – a large number of them are
aimed squarely at visitors, so standards can be patchy, especially
around Piazza della Signoria and Piazza del Duomo. But several
good-quality and good-value restaurants lie on the periphery of
the city centre, notably around **Santa Croce** and **Sant'Ambrogio**,
and across the river in **Oltrarno**. Simple meals are served in many
Florentine bars and cafés, so if you fancy a quick bite to eat rather
than a full-blown meal, take a look at our list of cafés and bars in
each Places chapter of this guide.
OUR FAVOURITES: Ora d'Aria, see page 51; Io – Osteria Personale, see page 108;
Il Guscio, see page 107.

Drink

As elsewhere in Italy, the distinction between Florentine bars and
cafés can be tricky to the point of impossibility, as almost every café
serves alcohol and almost every bar serves coffee. That said, some
cafés have an emphasis on coffee and cakes, just as there are plenty
of bars dedicated to the **wines** of the Tuscan vineyards. The humblest
wine bars belong to the endangered species known as the **vinaio**,
which consists of little more than a few shelves of workaday wines
plus a counter of snacks. At the opposite pole there's the **enoteca**,
which has a vast wine menu and often a good kitchen too.
OUR FAVOURITES: Fuori Porta, see page 105; Rex Caffè, see page 89; Volume, see
page 106.

Go out

Many of Florence's bars try to keep the punters on the premises by
serving free snacks with the **aperitivi** (usually about 7–9pm) before
the music kicks in – either live or (more often) supplied by a DJ.
Florence is generally a fairly sedate city, but it has some decent clubs
and music venues. For **information** about what's on, pick up a copy of
the *Firenze Spettacolo* monthly listings magazine.
OUR FAVOURITES: Tenax, see page 113; YAB, see page 65; Blob Club, see page 51.

Florence at a glance

Fortezza da Basso

VIALE SPARTA

West of the centre p.52.
On the west side of the central zone you'll find
Florence's big-money shopping street,
Via de'Tornabuoni. Beyond here, the big draw
is Santa Maria Novella, but there's plenty
more to see, notably Ognissanti, Santa Trìnita
and the Musei Marino Marini.

Stazione
Santa Maria
Novella

Mercato
Centrale

Santa Maria
Novella

San Lorenzo

Ognissanti

Museo
Novecento

Museo
Marino
Marini

Baptistery

VIA DE'TORNABUONI

Piazza del Duomo and around p.26.
Florence is a twin-nucleus city: one part for
the church, one part for the city authorities.
Piazza del Duomo, with the stupendous
cathedral, baptistery and bell tower, plus
the superb Museo dell'Opera del Duomo,
is the church's domain.

Palazzo
Strozzi

PIAZZA
DELLA
REPUBBLICA

Santa
Trìnita

River Arno

PIAZZA DEL
CARMINE

Santa Maria
del Carmine

Santo
Spirito

Santa
Felicita

Oltrarno p.92.
Oltrarno, squeezed between the hills and the
south bank of the river, has the city's biggest
concentration of good bars and restaurants,
especially around Piazza Santo Spirito and
Piazza del Carmine. Culturally, it's a rich area
too: in addition to Palazzo Pitti, you shouldn't
miss the churches of Santo Spirito and San
Miniato, nor the frescoes of the Cappella
Brancacci, one of Italy's greatest treasures.

OLTRARNO

Palazzo
Pitti

Forte di
Belvedere

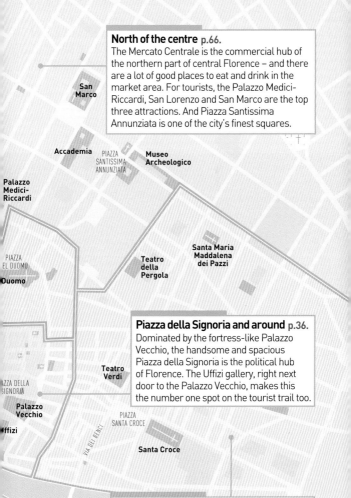

North of the centre p.66.

The Mercato Centrale is the commercial hub of the northern part of central Florence – and there are a lot of good places to eat and drink in the market area. For tourists, the Palazzo Medici-Riccardi, San Lorenzo and San Marco are the top three attractions. And Piazza Santissima Annunziata is one of the city's finest squares.

Piazza della Signoria and around p.36.

Dominated by the fortress-like Palazzo Vecchio, the handsome and spacious Piazza della Signoria is the political hub of Florence. The Uffizi gallery, right next door to the Palazzo Vecchio, makes this the number one spot on the tourist trail too.

East of the centre p.82.

To the east the centre of gravity is the spacious Piazza Santa Croce, with its mighty church. In the evening, the bars and restaurants of this quarter make it one of the liveliest parts of town. For the under-30s, the bars of Via dei Benci are always a big draw. You'll also find some of the city's best gelato and pizzas here, alongside the priciest haute cuisine in the city.

Things not to miss

It's not possible to see everything Florence has to offer in one trip – and we don't suggest you try. What follows is a selective taste of the city's highlights, from cultural and historic to the best places to eat and drink.

< The Museo dell'Opera del Duomo
See page 31
Ghiberti's "Gates of Paradise" plus masterpieces by Donatello and Michelangelo are on show in the Museo dell'Opera del Duomo.

∨ The Cappella Brancacci
See page 100
The startling images created by Masaccio make the Brancacci chapel one of the most significant artistic monuments in Europe.

< Santa Maria Novella
See page 59
Alberti's innovative facade
fronts this art-packed church,
featuring stunning frescoes by
Uccello, Ghirlandaio, Masaccio
and others.

∨ The Palazzo Medici-Riccardi
See page 71
Benozzo Gozzoli's delightful
frescoes are the highlight of the
huge Palazzo Medici-Riccardi.

THINGS NOT TO MISS

∧ **Uffizi**
See page 40
The Uffizi is undoubtedly the finest gathering of Italian Renaissance art on the planet.

< **San Lorenzo**
See page 66
The parish church of the Medici features some extraordinary Donatello sculptures.

∧ **Santa Croce**
See page 82
Glorious frescoes by Giotto and the serene Pazzi chapel are but two of the treasures of the mighty Santa Croce.

∨ **San Miniato al Monte**
See page 102
Overlooking the city from the south, the San Miniato is a masterpiece of Romanesque architecture.

∧ **Palazzo Pitti**
See page 93
The Palatina art collection is
second only to the Uffizi, and it's
just one of the museums to be
found in the colossal Pitti palace;
and the palace's garden – the
Bóboli – is gorgeous too.

< **The Palazzo Vecchio**
See page 38
Take one of the "Secret Tours" to
get the most out of the building
from which Florence was
governed.

< **Mercato Centrale**
See page 71
A cornucopia of local produce, with plenty of places to eat and drink upstairs.

∨ **The Accademia**
See page 73
Well, you can't come to Florence and not see the *David*, can you? Be sure to book your ticket in advance – there's always a queue to gaze at this most famous of sculptures.

Day one in Florence

The Uffizi see page 40. The Uffizi is the obvious first stop: a mind-blowing parade of masterpieces, and it now has 14 new rooms which focus on works by women and people of colour. If you're going in high season, make sure you book your ticket in advance or you face interminable queues.

Santa Croce see page 82. The vast church of Santa Croce has amazing frescoes by Giotto and other masters, and the Pazzi Chapel is one of the finest pieces of Renaissance architecture in Italy.

🍽️ **Lunch in Sant'Ambrogio** Grab a bargain lunch in the market (see page 88) – perhaps some salami, cheeses and biscotti – or drop in on Florence's best pizzeria, *Il Pizzaiuolo* (see page 91).

Ponte Vecchio see page 92. Take the picturesque route over the river into the Oltrarno district.

Palazzo Pitti see page 93. You could spend all day in the Pitti, which has several museums under its roofs – the Palatina galleries are the absolute highlight, with wonderful paintings by Raphael, Titian and many others. The palace's garden is wonderful too.

Cappella Brancacci see page 100. Masaccio's frescoes are epoch-defining creations.

🍽️ **Dinner** at *Oliviero 1962* (see page 65), followed by a nightcap at *Zoe* (see page 106) or *Il Rifrullo* (see page 105).

Santa Croce

Ponte Vecchio

Zoe

Day two in Florence

The Bargello see page 44. Get a crash-course in Renaissance sculpture: Michelangelo, Cellini, Donatello, Verrocchio – they're all here.

The Duomo see page 26. The dome of the Duomo is one of the most incredible structures in all of Italy.

The Museo dell'Opera del Duomo see page 31. Michelangelo's harrowing *Pietà*, a roomful of wonderful Donatellos, the *Doors of Paradise*, and much more.

Lunch *Yellow Bar* (see page 51). It may not look like much, but *Yellow Bar* is one of the best places in the city for an unpretentious meal.

San Lorenzo and Medici tombs see page 66. There's yet more from Michelangelo and Donatello at the mausoleum of Florence's quasi-royal family – and don't miss the amazing library next door.

Santa Maria Novella and its museum see page 59. Alberti's facade makes Santa Maria Novella perhaps the city's most handsome church, and a cornucopia of memorable art is to be found inside, including an exquisite fresco cycle by Ghirlandaio.

Aperitivo Cross the water for a drink at *La Cité* (see page 105) then stroll over to the chic and innovative *Io – Osteria Personale* (see page 108), one of the most interesting restaurants.

The Duomo

Santa Maria Novella

Yellow Bar

Quiet Florence

Florence is one of Europe's busiest tourist destinations, but it's possible to escape the crowds. These places are rarely busy, and in low season you could have them to yourself.

Museo Galileo see page 43. Everybody knows about the art, but few visitors bother themselves with Florence's scientific heritage – this fascinating museum fills in the story.

Santi Apostoli see page 53. This beautiful and ancient church is the most tranquil building in central Florence.

Santa Trìnita see page 56. One of the chapels here has a gorgeous cycle of frescoes by Ghirlandaio.

Ognissanti see page 62. It has a Giotto painting, a Botticelli and two works by Ghirlandaio, but Ognissanti is overlooked by the tour groups.

Museo Galileo

Lunch Buy your supplies at an *alimentari*, and wander out to the Cascine park (see page 110) for a picnic lunch.

Santo Spirito see page 98. Don't be deterred by the blank exterior – Brunelleschi's spacious and serene church is a marvel of Renaissance design.

Santa Felìcita see page 92. Located just yards from the Ponte Vecchio, Santa Felìcita demands a visit for Pontormo's extraordinary *Deposition*.

San Miniato al Monte see page 102. Climb the hill to visit this glorious Romanesque church, perhaps the most serene building in the city.

Evening in Oltrarno see page 105. When it comes to eating and drinking, you're spoilt for choice on Florence's south bank but if it's a tranquil evening you're after, avoid Piazza Santo Spirito.

Santi Apostoli

San Miniato al Monte

Shopping Florence

The hometown of Gucci, Pucci and Ferragamo has plenty of outlets that cater for gold-card holders, as you'd expect, but there are also places to tempt those on a tighter budget.

Coin and Rinascente see pages 49 and 35. Explore the city's two major department stores, finishing with a coffee on the roof of Rinascente.

San Lorenzo Market see page 80. The avenues of market stalls at San Lorenzo will keep you browsing for a while, and the food hall is irresistible.

 Lunch *Da Mario* (see page 81), located just yards from the market hall, is a real Florentine institution.

Farmacia di Santa Maria Novella see page 63. Florence's most gorgeous (and aromatic) shop is worth a visit just to inhale the heavily fragranced air.

Via de' Tornabuoni see page 57. Even if you can't afford a Pucci frock, window-shopping is fun on the city's designer row.

Giulio Giannini e Figlio see page 104. Pick up a souvenir at this long-established maker of marbled paper and notebooks.

Scuola del Cuoio see page 88. Leather is a real Florentine speciality. Cross town to check out the biggest outlet for well-made and well-priced bags and belts.

 Evening around Santa Croce and Sant'Ambrogio *Cibrèo* (see page 90) is one of the best restaurants in this part of town.

Farmacia di Santa Maria Novella

San Lorenzo Market

Scuola del Cuoio

Florence viewpoints

Florence is one of the most photogenic cities in Europe, and it's dotted with places that give you a great view of the townscape.

Brunelleschi's dome see page 29. You could start the day by surveying the centre of the city from the summit of Brunelleschi's dome. Or, if the queue is too long, climb the adjacent Campanile instead.

Forte di Belvedere see page 96. The Forte di Belvedere is open whenever it's in use as an exhibition space. If it's open when you're in town, be sure to visit – the view is terrific, and it's rarely as busy as Piazzale Michelangelo, a well-known vantage point on the neighbouring hill.

Villa Bardini see page 102. The Villa Bardini often has excellent exhibitions, and the tiny third-floor terrace gives you an unforgettable panorama.

🍴 **Lunch** see pages 105 and 106. Stop for a light lunch – and a glass of fine wine – at *Fuori Porta* or *Le Volpi e l'Uva*.

Fiesole see page 114. In the afternoon take a bus up to the hilltop village of Fiesole. It's an attractive little place, and the whole of Florence is spread out below.

🍴 **Dinner** see page 117. At the end of the day, eat at *La Reggia degli Etruschi* or *Terrazza 45*, and watch the sun go down over the city.

View from the Villa Bardini

Fiesole

Le Volpi e l'Uva

Florence galleries

Of course you'll want to visit the big museums and galleries, but it's worth making time for some of the smaller and quirkier collections too.

La Specola see page 97. This is the oddest museum in the city – a collection of anatomical waxworks of dazzling accuracy and gruesome beauty.

The Museo Stefano Bardini see page 101. The private art collection of Stefano Bardini, housed in the vast rooms of his former home, is displayed more or less as he left it.

The Museo Horne see page 87. On the other side of the river, the collection of Herbert Percy Horne is displayed in a lovely old house that's a delight in itself.

Museo Marino Marini

Lunch see page 91. Have lunch at the ever-popular *Osteria Caffè Italiano*, just a five-minute walk from the Horne museum, or at one of the host of other restaurants around Santa Croce.

The Museo dell'Opificio delle Pietre Dure see page 74. The art of stone inlay is a Florentine speciality – the objects are not to everyone's taste, but the skill involved in their creation is astonishing.

The Museo Marino Marini see page 58. A large and well-displayed collection of work by one of Italy's best-known modern artists – plus Alberti's exquisite Ruccellai chapel.

La Specola

Dinner and drinks see pages 64 and 51. After an aperitivo at the *Art Bar*, treat yourself to a meal at *Ora d'Aria*, one of the city's best restaurants.

Art Bar

PLACES

The inner courtyard at the Palazzo Vecchio

Piazza del Duomo and around

All first-time visitors gravitate towards Piazza del Duomo, beckoned by the pinnacle of Brunelleschi's dome, which lords over the cityscape with an authority unmatched by any architectural creation in any other Italian city. Yet even though the magnitude of the Duomo is apparent from a distance, the first sight of the cathedral and the adjacent Baptistery still comes as a delightful jolt, their colourful patterned exteriors making a startling contrast with the sand-toned buildings around. Once you've finished exploring these mighty monuments, the obvious next step is to visit the superb Museo dell'Opera del Duomo, a vast repository for works of art removed over the centuries from the Duomo, Baptistery and Campanile.

The Duomo

MAP PAGE 28, POCKET MAP C10–D10
Piazza del Duomo.
Ⓦ operaduomo.firenze.it. Free, joint tickets available including other sights.

Some time in the seventh century the seat of the Bishop of Florence was transferred from San Lorenzo to Santa Reparata, a sixth-century church which stood on the site of the present-day **Duomo**, or **Santa Maria del Fiore** to give it its full name. Later generations modified this older church until 1294, when Arnolfo di Cambio drafted a scheme to create the largest church in the Catholic world. Progress on the project faltered after Arnolfo's death in 1302, but by 1418 only

View from the Campanile of the Duomo

Duomo passes

There are three different passes to the major points of interest in Piazza del Duomo, and all are available at Ⓦ duomo.firenze.it. All passes allow one entry to selected sights and each pass lasts three days. The Ghiberti Pass allows access to the Baptistery, the Museo dell'Opera del Duomo and Santa Reparata; the Giotto Pass includes all of the above as well as the Campanile; and the Brunelleschi Pass also adds in the dome.

the dome – no small matter – remained unfinished.

Parts of the Duomo's **exterior** date back to Arnolfo's era, but most of the overblown main façade is a nineteenth-century pseudo-Gothic front. The most attractive external feature is the **Porta della Mandorla** on the north side. This doorway takes its name from the almond-shaped frame (*mandorla* means almond) that contains *The Assumption of the Virgin* (1414–21), sculpted by Nanni di Banco.

The Duomo's **interior** is a vast, uncluttered enclosure of bare masonry, alleviated by a pair of frescoed memorials to *condottieri* (mercenary commanders) on the north side of the nave: Paolo Uccello's monument to Sir John Hawkwood, created in 1436, and Andrea del Castagno's monument to Niccolò da Tolentino, painted twenty years later. Just beyond the horsemen, Domenico di Michelino's 1465 *Dante Explaining the Divine Comedy* gives Brunelleschi's dome – then nearing completion – a place only marginally less prominent than the mountain of Purgatory.

Barriers usually prevent visitors from going any further, but you might be able to take a look into the **Sagrestia Nuova**, where the lavish panelling is inlaid with beautiful intarsia work (1436–45) by Benedetto and Giuliano Maiano. The mighty sacristy door (1445–69), created in conjunction with Michelozzo, was Luca della Robbia's only work in bronze. It

was in this sacristy that Lorenzo de' Medici took refuge in 1478 after his brother Giuliano had been mortally stabbed on the altar steps by the Pazzi conspirators (see page 30); the bulk of the recently installed doors protected him from his would-be assassins. Small portraits on the handles commemorate the brothers.

In the 1960s, remnants of the Duomo's predecessor, **Santa Reparata** were uncovered underneath the west end of the nave. Subsequent diggings have revealed a jigsaw of Roman, Paleochristian and Romanesque remains, plus fragments of mosaic and fourteenth-century frescoes and Brunelleschi's tomb, a marble slab so unassuming that it had lain forgotten under the south aisle.

Climbing the **dome** is an amazing experience, both for the views from the top and for the insights it offers into Brunelleschi's engineering genius (see page 29). Visits are timed and booking in advance is essential; even so, be prepared to queue, and be ready for the 463 lung-busting steps. It's worth it, though.

The Campanile

MAP PAGE 28, POCKET MAP C10
Piazza del Duomo.
Ⓦ operaduomo.firenze.it. Charge, joint tickets available including other sights.
The **Campanile** was begun in 1334 by Giotto during his period as official city architect and *capo maestro* (head of works) in charge of the Duomo. By the time of his death three years later, the base,

the first of five eventual levels, had been completed. Andrea Pisano, fresh from creating the Baptistery's south doors (see page 29), continued construction of the second storey (1337–42), probably in accordance with Giotto's plans. Work was rounded off by Francesco Talenti, who rectified deficiencies in Giotto's original calculations in the process: the base's original walls teetered on the brink of collapse until he doubled their thickness. When completed, the bell tower reached 84.7m, well over the limit set by the city in 1324 for civic towers.

The tower's decorative **sculptures and reliefs** – they are copies; the originals are in the Museo dell'Opera del Duomo (see page 31) – illustrate humanity's progress from original sin to a state of divine grace, a progress facilitated by manual labour, the arts and the sacraments, and

guided by the influence of the planets and the cardinal and theological virtues.

A climb to the summit is one of the highlights of any Florentine trip: the parapet at the top of the tower is a less lofty but in many ways more satisfying viewpoint than the cathedral dome, if only because the view takes in the dome itself. There are 414 steps to the summit – and there's no lift.

The Baptistery

MAP PAGE 28, POCKET MAP C10
Piazza del Duomo.
ⓦ operaduomo.firenze.it. Charge, joint tickets available including other sights.

Generally thought to date from the sixth or seventh century, the **Baptistery** is the **oldest building** in Florence, and was first documented in 897, when it was the city's cathedral.

The Florentines were always conscious of their Roman ancestry,

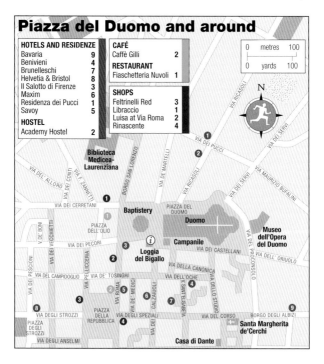

Piazza del Duomo and around

HOTELS AND RESIDENCE	
Bavaria	9
Benivieni	4
Brunelleschi	7
Helvetia & Bristol	8
Il Salotto di Firenze	3
Maxim	6
Residenza dei Pucci	1
Savoy	5
HOSTEL	
Academy Hostel	2

CAFÉ	
Caffè Gilli	2
RESTAURANT	
Fiaschetteria Nuvoli	1

SHOPS	
Feltrinelli Red	3
Libraccio	1
Luisa at Via Roma	2
Rinascente	4

0 metres 100
0 yards 100

Brunelleschi's dome

Since Arnolfo di Cambio's model of the Duomo collapsed some time in the fourteenth century, nobody has been sure quite how he intended to crown his achievement. In 1367 Neri di Fioraventi proposed the construction of a magnificent cupola that was to span nearly 43m, broader than the dome of Rome's Pantheon, which had been the world's largest for 1300 years.

There was just one problem: nobody had worked out how to build such a thing. Medieval arches were usually built on wooden "centring", a network of timbers that held the stone in place until the mortar was set. In the case of the Duomo, the weight of the stone would have been too great for the timber. Eventually the project was thrown open to competition, and a goldsmith and clockmaker, Filippo Brunelleschi, presented the winning scheme. The key to Brunelleschi's success lay in the construction of the dome as two masonry shells, each built as a stack of ever-diminishing rings. Secured with hidden stone beams and enormous iron chains, these concentric circles formed a lattice that was filled with lightweight bricks laid in a herringbone pattern that prevented the higher sections from falling inwards.

The dome's completion was marked by the consecration of the cathedral on March 25, 1436 – Annunciation Day, and the Florentine New Year – in a ceremony conducted by the pope. Even then, the topmost piece, the lantern, remained unfinished, with many people convinced the dome could support no further weight. But once again Brunelleschi won the day, beginning work on the dome's final stage in 1446, just a few months before his death. The whole thing was finally completed in the late 1460s, when the cross and gilded ball, both cast by Verrocchio, were hoisted into place. It is still the largest masonry dome in the world.

and for centuries believed that the Baptistery was a converted Roman temple to Mars. This isn't the case, but its exterior marble cladding – applied between about 1059 and 1128 – is clearly classical in inspiration, while its most famous embellishments, the gilded **bronze doors**, mark the emergence of a more scholarly, self-conscious interest in the art of the ancient world.

The arrival of Andrea Pisano in Florence in 1330 offered the chance to outdo the celebrated bronze portals of arch-rival Pisa's cathedral. Most of the **south doors'** 28 panels, installed in 1339, form a narrative on the life of St John the Baptist, patron saint of Florence and the Baptistery's dedicatee. In 2019, replicas replaced the originals, which have been moved to the Museo dell'Opera del Duomo.

Some sixty years of financial and political turmoil, and the ravages of the Black Death, prevented further work on the Baptistery's other entrances until 1401. That year a competition was held to design a new set of doors, with the entrants being asked to create a panel showing *The Sacrifice of Isaac*. The judges found themselves equally impressed by the work of two young goldsmiths, **Brunelleschi** and

The Pazzi Conspiracy

The Pazzi Conspiracy had its roots in the election in 1472 of Pope Sixtus IV, who promptly made six of his nephews cardinals. One of them, Girolamo Riario, received particularly preferential treatment, probably because he was in fact Sixtus's son. Sixtus's plan was that Riario should take over the town of Imola as a base for papal expansion, and accordingly he approached Lorenzo de' Medici for the necessary loan. When Lorenzo rebuffed him, and in addition refused to recognize Francesco Salviati as archbishop of Pisa, a furious Sixtus turned to the Pazzi, the Medici's leading Florentine rivals as bankers in Rome.

Three co-conspirators met in Rome in the early months of 1477: Riario, now in possession of Imola but eager for greater spoils; Salviati, incandescent at Lorenzo's veto; and Francesco de' Pazzi, head of the Pazzi's Rome operation and determined to usurp Medici power in Florence. After numerous false starts, it was decided to murder Lorenzo and Giuliano while they attended Mass in Florence's cathedral. The date set was Sunday, April 26, 1478: Lorenzo's extermination was delegated to two embittered priests, Maffei and Bagnone, whereas Giuliano was to be dispatched by Francesco de' Pazzi and Bernardo Baroncelli, a Pazzi sidekick.

It all went horribly wrong. Giuliano was killed, but Lorenzo managed to escape, fleeing wounded to the Duomo's new sacristy. The conspirators were soon dealt with: Salviati and Francesco de' Pazzi were hanged from a window of the Palazzo della Signoria; Maffei and Bagnone were castrated and hanged; Baroncelli escaped to Constantinople but was extradited and executed; and Jacopo de' Pazzi, the godfather of the Pazzi clan, was tortured, hanged alongside the decomposing Salviati and finally hurled into the river.

Lorenzo Ghiberti; both winning entries are displayed in the Bargello (see page 44). Unable to choose between the pair, the judges suggested that they work in tandem. Brunelleschi replied that if he couldn't do the job alone he wasn't interested – whereupon the contract was handed to Ghiberti.

His **north doors** (1403–24) show a new naturalism and classicized sense of composition, but they are as nothing to the gilded **east doors** (1425–52), which have long been known as the "Gates of Paradise", supposedly because Michelangelo once remarked that they were so beautiful they deserved to be the portals of heaven. These are copies – the originals are in the Museo dell'Opera del Duomo (see page 31).

The Baptistery **interior** is stunning, with its black and white marble cladding and miscellany of ancient columns below a blazing thirteenth-century mosaic ceiling, dominated by Christ in Judgement. The interior's semi-abstract mosaic pavement also dates from the thirteenth century. The empty octagon at its centre marks the spot once occupied by the huge font in which every child born in the city during the previous twelve months would be baptized on March 25 (New Year's Day in the old Florentine calendar). To the right of the altar lies the tomb of Baldassare Cossa, the schismatic Pope John

XXIII, who was deposed in 1415 and died in Florence in 1419.

A campaign to restore the stunning mosaics began in February 2023; total restoration of all 10 million tiles is expected to take six years to complete. The campaign could present a unique opportunity to see the Baptistery's interior up close – there has been talk of allowing guided visits on the scaffolding where the restorers are working. Even if this doesn't come to pass, the Baptistery will remain open to visitors during this time, though be aware that some of the mosaics may be obscured from view.

The Museo dell'Opera del Duomo

MAP PAGE 28, POCKET MAP D10
Piazza del Duomo. Ⓦ operaduomo.firenze.
it. Charge, included in joint ticket also covering other sights.

In 1296 a body called the Opera del Duomo ("Work of the Duomo") was created to oversee the maintenance of the Duomo. Since the early fifteenth century its home has been the building behind the east end of the cathedral at Piazza del Duomo 9, which also houses the superb **Museo dell'Opera del Duomo**.

The collection comprises more than 750 items arrayed over three floors, as a €50 million rebuild in 2015 saw the museum extended into an adjacent eighteenth-century theatre. The show-stopper on the ground floor is a huge top-lit hall containing a reconstruction of **Arnolfo di Cambio**'s facade of the Duomo. Nearly 40m wide and 20m tall, the replica is adorned with many of the sculptures that occupied the facade's various niches before it was dismantled in 1587. Arnolfo and his workshop produced the eerily glass-eyed *Madonna and Child*; equally striking are his *St Reparata*, one of Florence's patron

The Museo dell'Opera del Duomo

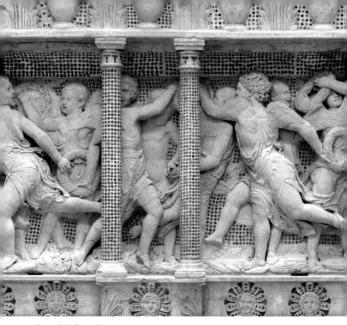

Donatello's *Cantoria*

saints, and the ramrod-straight statue of Boniface VIII, whose corruption earned him a place in Dante's *Inferno*, which was partly written during Boniface's pontificate. Of the four seated figures of the Evangelists, Nanni di Banco's *St Luke* and Donatello's *St John* are particularly fine. Facing the facade are **Ghiberti**'s stupendous gilded bronze "Doors of Paradise" and the Baptistery's original North Doors, also created by Ghiberti. These will soon be joined by the originals of Andrea Pisano's South Doors.

Also on the ground floor you'll find a room devoted to **Michelangelo**'s anguished *Pietà* (1550–53), which was removed from the cathedral in 1981. Carved when he was almost 80, this is one of his last works, and was intended for his own tomb; Vasari records that the face of Nicodemus is a self-portrait. Dissatisfied with the quality of the marble, Michelangelo mutilated the group by hammering off the left leg and arm of Christ; a

pupil restored the arm, then finished off the figure of Mary Magdalene.

In the adjacent room the greatest of Michelangelo's precursors, **Donatello**, provides the focus with a gaunt wooden figure of Mary Magdalene (1453–55), created for the Baptistery. The adjoining octagonal chapel features an assembly of reliquaries which contain, among other saintly remains, the jaw of Saint Jerome and an index finger of John the Baptist.

There are more masterpieces by Donatello upstairs, where the long Galleria del Campanile – which overlooks the di Cambio facade – is lined with sixteen life-sized sculptures and 54 bas-relief panels from the Campanile. Five of the large figures are by Donatello, with perhaps the most powerful of them being the prophet Habbakuk, the intensity of whose gaze is said to have prompted the sculptor to seize it and yell, "Speak, speak!" Keeping company with Donatello's work are four

Prophets (1348–50) and two Sibyls (1342–48) attributed to Andrea Pisano, and *The Sacrifice of Isaac* (1421), a collaboration between Nanni di Bartolo and Donatello. The gallery's bas-reliefs depict the spiritual refinement of humanity through labour, the arts and, ultimately, the virtues and sacraments. The key panels are the hexagonal reliefs from the lower tier, all of which – save for the last five, by Luca della Robbia (1437–39) – were the work of **Andrea Pisano** and his son Nino (c.1348–50), probably to designs by Giotto.

Donatello's magnificent *cantoria*, or choir loft (1433–39), with its playground of boisterous putti, hangs on the wall of another spacious room; on the opposite wall is the *cantoria* created by the young Luca della Robbia (the original panels are displayed below the *cantoria*, with casts replacing them in the loft itself). In the Sala del Tesoro you'll find an amazing **silver altar-front** that's covered with scenes from the life of St John the Baptist. Begun in 1366, this mighty piece was completed in 1480, the culmination of a century of labour by, among others, Michelozzo, Antonio del Pollaiuolo and Verrocchio. Next door there's a sequence of marble reliefs by Bacio Bandinelli and Giovanni Bandini, part of an unfinished sequence of three hundred panels proposed for the cathedral choir.

On the top floor are displayed designs for the Duomo's facade. The itinerary ends on a panoramic terrace offering a terrific view of Brunelleschi's dome.

Piazza della Repubblica

MAP PAGE 28, POCKET MAP B11

A short distance to the south of Piazza del Duomo, the vacant expanse of **Piazza della Repubblica** opens up. Impressive solely for its size, this square was planned in the late 1860s, as part of Giuseppe Poggi's masterplan for the capital of the recently formed

Piazza della Repubblica

Florence – the capital of Italy

At the start of 1865 Florence became the first capital of the newly united Italy. It was to hold this position for only five years, but during this period a transformation of the city was begun, following a plan conceived by Giuseppe Poggi (1811–1901). The city walls were demolished, and wide boulevards or *viali* put in their place; shopping streets such as Via de' Cerretani and Via de' Tornabuoni were widened and modernized; the riverbanks were developed; and Piazzale Michelangelo was created on the hill of San Miniato. But the most drastic intervention in the city centre was the removal of the old market and the surrounding slums – a new market hall was built near San Lorenzo, and the ancient market area became Piazza della Repubblica.

Italian nation. However, the clearance of the **Mercato Vecchio** had not even begun when the capital was transferred to Rome, and it wasn't until 1885 that the marketplace and its disease-ridden tenements were finally swept away. On the west side a vast **arch** bears the triumphant inscription: "The ancient city centre restored to new life from the squalor of centuries."

The free-standing column is the solitary trace of the piazza's history. Once surrounded by stalls, it used to be topped by Donatello's statue of *Abundance*, and a bell that was rung to signal the start and close of trading. Nowadays, Piazza della Repubblica is best known for the three large and expensive **cafés** that stand on the perimeter: the *Gilli* (see page 35); the *Giubbe Rosse*, where the Futurist manifesto was launched in 1909; and the *Paszkowski*, which began business as a beer hall in the 1840s.

Mercato Vecchio

Shops

Feltrinelli Red

MAP PAGE 28, POCKET MAP B11
Piazza della Repubblica 27r.
Ⓦ lafeltrinelli.it.
The *Feltrinelli Red* format –
combining a multi-floor bookshop
with a café-restaurant (*Red* stands
for "read, eat, dream") – was
pioneered in Rome and has now
found a loyal contingent of local
customers in Florence. The stock
is more impressive at the city's
other main Feltrinelli branch,
which you can find nearby at Via
de' Cerretani 40.

Libraccio

MAP PAGE 28, POCKET MAP B10
Via de' Cerretani 16r. Ⓦ ibs.it.
Florence's branch of the nationwide
Libraccio is the biggest bookshop in
the city – it's enormous, and has a
good selection of English-language
books.

Luisa at Via Roma

MAP PAGE 28, POCKET MAP B10
Via Roma 19–21r. Ⓦ luisaviaroma.com.
Luisa was founded back in the
1930s and remains Florence's top-
end multi-label clothes shop. The
interior is one of Florence's more
impressive examples of modern
architectural design.

Rinascente

MAP PAGE 28, POCKET MAP C11
Piazza della Repubblica 1 Ⓦ rinascente.it.
Like Coin (see page 49),
Rinascente is part of a countrywide
chain, though this store is a touch
more upmarket than its nearby
rival, and bigger, with six floors of
clothes, linen, cosmetics and other
household items. The rooftop café
gives a great view of the Duomo.

Café

Caffè Gilli

MAP PAGE 28, POCKET MAP B11

Cantucci at Caffè Gilli

Via Roma 1r. Ⓦ caffegilli.com.
This is the most appealing of Piazza
della Repubblica's expensive cafés.
It was founded in 1733 and has
a lavish Belle Epoque interior.
Their famous hot chocolate, which
comes in five blended flavours,
is an absolute must on chilly
afternoons. €

Restaurant

Fiaschetteria Nuvoli

MAP PAGE 28, POCKET MAP B10
Piazza dell'Olio 15. ☏ 055 239 6616.
For a basic meal within a stone's
throw of the Duomo, you can't
do better than this. Upstairs,
the tiny, dark, bottle-lined bar
is dominated by a counter laden
with cold meats, *crostini* and
other snacks. In the basement,
good-value Florentine staples are
served at half a dozen communal
tables. €

Piazza della Signoria and around

Whereas the Piazza del Duomo provides the focus for the city's religious life, the Piazza della Signoria – site of the magnificent Palazzo Vecchio and forecourt to the Uffizi gallery – has always been the centre of its secular existence. Created in 1307 to provide a setting for the Palazzo Vecchio, the piazza was paved by 1385 and reached its present-day dimensions in 1871, after Florence's brief spell as the capital of the country. The dense network of streets northeast of the Piazza della Signoria is dominated by the campanile of the Badìa Fiorentina, the most important of several buildings in the area that have the strongest associations with Dante Alighieri. Immediately opposite the church stands the forbidding bulk of the Bargello, once the city's prison, now home to a superb collection of sculpture and objets d'art. To the south of the Bargello, at the back of the Uffizi, lies the fascinating Museo Galileo, a sight too often overlooked by art-obsessed visitors. The main catwalk of the Florentine passeggiata is Via dei Calzaiuoli, the broad avenue that links Piazza della Signoria with Piazza del Duomo. Shop-lined for most of its length, it boasts one stupendous monument, the church of Orsanmichele.

The Piazza della Signoria statues

MAP PAGE 38, POCKET MAP C12

Florence's political volatility is encapsulated by the Piazza della Signoria's array of **statues**. From left to right, the line-up starts with Giambologna's equestrian statue (1587–94) of Cosimo I; mimicking the famous Marcus Aurelius statue in Rome, it was designed to draw parallels between the power of medieval Florence (and thus Cosimo) and the glory of imperial Rome.

Next comes Ammannati's fatuous **Neptune** fountain (1565–75), a tribute to Cosimo's prowess as a naval commander. Neptune himself is a lumpen lout of a figure, who provoked Michelangelo to coin the rhyming put-down *Ammannato, Ammannato, che bel marmo hai rovinato* ("…what a fine piece of marble you've ruined"). After a copy of Donatello's *Marzocco* (1418–20), the original of which is in the Bargello, comes a replica of the same sculptor's *Judith and Holofernes* (1456–60), which freezes the action at the moment Judith's arm begins its scything stroke – a dramatic conception that no other sculptor of the period would have attempted. Commissioned by Cosimo de' Medici, this statue doubled as a fountain in the Palazzo Medici but was removed to the Piazza della

Signoria after the expulsion of the family in 1495, to be displayed as an emblem of vanquished tyranny; the original is in the Palazzo Vecchio.

Michelangelo's *David*, at first intended for the Duomo, was also installed here in 1504 as a declaration of civic solidarity by the Florentine Republic; the original is now cooped up in the Accademia (see page 73). Bandinelli's adjacent *Hercules and Cacus* (1534) was designed as a personal emblem of Cosimo I and a symbol of Florentine fortitude. Benvenuto Cellini described the muscle-bound Hercules as looking like "a sackful of melons".

The Loggia della Signoria

MAP PAGE 38, POCKET MAP C12–C13

The square's grace note, the **Loggia della Signoria**, was completed in 1382 and served as a dais for city dignitaries, a forum for meeting foreign emissaries and a platform for the swearing-in of public officials. Its alternative name, the Loggia dei Lanzi, comes from Cosimo I's bodyguard of Swiss lancers, who were garrisoned nearby.

Although Donatello's *Judith and Holofernes* was placed here as early as 1506, it was only in the late eighteenth century that the loggia became exclusively a **showcase** for sculpture. In the corner nearest the Palazzo Vecchio stands a figure that has become one of the iconic images of the Renaissance, Benvenuto Cellini's *Perseus* (1554). Made for Cosimo I, the statue symbolizes the triumph of firm grand ducal rule over the monstrous indiscipline of all other forms of government. Equally attention-seeking is Giambologna's last work, to the right, *The Rape of the Sabine* (1583), the epitome of the Mannerist obsession with spiralling forms. The sculptor intended the piece merely as a study of old age, male strength and female beauty; the present name was coined after the event. The figures along the back wall are Roman works, traditionally believed to portray empresses, while of the three central statues only one – Giambologna's *Hercules Slaying the Centaur* (1599) – deserves such prominence.

The Neptune fountain, Piazza della Signoria

Gucci Garden

MAP PAGE 38, POCKET MAP D12
Piazza della Signoria 10.
Ⓦ bit.ly/GucciGardenIT. Charge.

The piazza's massive fourteenth-century Palazzo della Mercanzia now belongs to Gucci, Florence's most famous **fashion house**. Founded by Guccio Gucci in 1921, the company lost its way in the 1980s and the family was forced to sell to a Bahraini investment group. Having been rescued by the Midas touch of Tom Ford, the label is again one of Italy's coolest, and the redesigned interior of the palazzo has several rooms in which Gucci goods are displayed like timeless works of art. There's also the inevitable gift shop and a similarly exorbitant restaurant, run by a three-Michelin-star chef.

The Palazzo Vecchio

MAP PAGE 38, POCKET MAP C12–D13
Piazza della Signoria.
Ⓦ bit.ly/ThePalazzoVecchio. Charge.

Florence's fortress-like **town hall**, the **Palazzo Vecchio**, was begun in the last year of the thirteenth century, as the home of the *Priori*, or *Signoria*, the highest tier of the city's republican government (see page 39). In 1540 Cosimo I moved his retinue here from the Palazzo Medici and grafted a huge extension onto the rear of the building. The Medici remained in residence for only nine years before moving to the Palazzo Pitti – that's when the "old" (*vecchio*) palace acquired its present name.

The small – and free – **Tracce di Firenze** (Traces of Florence) museum, on the ground floor of the palazzo, is in essence a collection of maps, prints, photos and topographical paintings that chart the growth of Florence from the fifteenth century to the present. Perhaps the most impressive item is

GELATERIA
Perchè No!   3

RESTAURANTS
Antico Fattore   9
Gustavino   6
Ora d'Aria   12
Vini e Vecchi Sapori   7
Yellow Bar   1

CAFÉS, BARS AND SNACKS
All'Antico Vinaio   11
Brac   14
Cantinetta dei Verrazzano   2
I Fratellini   4
Il Cernacchino   5
'Ino   13
La Prosciutteria   10
Rivoire   8

SHOPS
Coin   3
Spezierie
Palazzo Vecchio   2
Torrini   1

HOTELS AND RESIDENZE
Hermitage   3
Relais Cavalcanti   2
Residenza d'Epoca
in Piazza della Signoria   1

CLUB
Blob Club   1

Piazza della Signoria and around

The Florentine Republic

Between 1293 and 1534 – bar the odd ruction – Florence maintained a republican constitution that was embodied in well-defined institutions. The rulers were drawn from the ranks of guild members over the age of 30, and were chosen in a public ceremony held every two months. At this ceremony, eight men were picked by lottery to become the *Priori* (or *Signori*), forming a government called the *Signoria*. Once elected, the *Priori* moved into the Palazzo della Signoria, where they stayed throughout their brief period of office.

Headed by the *Gonfaloniere* (the "Standard-Bearer"), the *Signoria* consulted two elected councils, or *Collegi*, as well as committees introduced to deal with specific crises. Permanent officials included the Chancellor (a post once held by Machiavelli) and the *Podestà*, a magistrate brought in from a neighbouring city as an independent arbitrator. In times of extreme crisis all male citizens over the age of 14 (apart from clerics) were summoned to a *Parlamento* in Piazza della Signoria. When a two-thirds quorum was reached, the people were asked to approve a *Balìa*, a committee to deal with the situation as it saw fit.

All this looked good on paper, but political cliques had few problems ensuring that only likely supporters found their way into the lottery process. If a rogue candidate slipped through the net, or things went awry, then a *Parlamento* was summoned, and the resulting *Balìa* replaced the offending person with a more pliable candidate. It was by such means that the mercantile dynasties – the Peruzzi, the Albizzi, the Strozzi and of course the Medici – retained their power even when not technically in office.

the meticulous nineteenth-century reproduction of a 1472 aerial view of Florence called the **Pianta della Catena** (Chain Map), the original of which was destroyed in Berlin during World War II.

Work on the beautiful inner **courtyard** was begun by Michelozzo in 1453; the decoration was largely added by Vasari on the occasion of Francesco de' Medici's marriage to Johanna of Austria in 1565.

Vasari was given full rein in the huge **Salone del Cinquecento** at the top of the stairs. The chamber might have had one of Italy's most remarkable decorative schemes: Leonardo da Vinci and Michelangelo were employed to paint frescoes on opposite sides of the room, but Leonardo's work, *The Battle of Anghiari*, was abandoned

after his experimental technique went wrong, while Michelangelo's *The Battle of Cascina* had not left the drawing board when he was summoned to Rome by Pope Julius II in 1506. Instead, the hall received six drearily bombastic murals (1563–65) – painted either by Vasari or under his direction – illustrating Florentine military triumphs over Pisa and Siena. It has generally been assumed that Vasari obliterated whatever remained of Leonardo's fresco before beginning his work, but the discovery of a cavity behind *The Battle of Marciano* has raised the possibility that Vasari instead constructed a false wall for his fresco, to preserve his great predecessor's painting. Investigations are proceeding.

The **sculptural highlight** is Michelangelo's *Victory*, almost opposite the entrance door. Carved for the tomb of Pope Julius II, the statue was donated to the Medici by the artist's nephew, then installed here by Vasari in 1565 to celebrate Cosimo's defeat of the Sienese ten years earlier. Directly opposite is the plaster model of a companion piece for the *Victory*, Giambologna's *Virtue Overcoming Vice*, another metaphor for Florentine military might.

From the Salone del Cinquecento, a roped-off door allows a glimpse of the most bizarre room in the building, the **Studiolo di Francesco I**. Designed by Vasari and decorated by no fewer than thirty Mannerist artists (1570–74), this windowless cell was created as a retreat for the introverted son of Cosimo and Eleanor, whose portraits face each other across the room.

Upstairs, in the six rooms of the Quartiere di Eleonora di Toledo, the star turn is the tiny and exquisite **Cappella di Eleonora**, vividly decorated in glassy Mannerist style by Bronzino in the 1540s. The **Sala dell'Udienza**, which was originally the audience chamber of the Republic, boasts a stunning gilt-coffered ceiling by Giuliano da Maiano, who was also responsible, with his brother Benedetto, for the intarsia work on the doors and the lovely doorway that leads into the **Sala dei Gigli**, a room that takes its name from the lilies (*gigli*) that adorn most of its surfaces. The room has another splendid ceiling by the Maiano

brothers, and a fresco by Domenico Ghirlandaio of *SS Zenobius, Stephen and Lorenzo* (1481–85), but the undoubted highlight here is Donatello's original *Judith and Holofernes* (1455–60).

Outside the Sala dei Gigli, a staircase leads to the **tower** of the Palazzo Vecchio (charge, or included with tours); a 223-step climb takes you to a terrace beneath the bell chambers, passing the prison cell known ironically as the Alberghinetto (Little Hotel), where Cosimo il Vecchio and Savonarola were both held.

The palazzo was built over an amphitheatre that was raised during the reign of Emperor Hadrian. The excavated ruins are open to the public by guided tour, which must be booked when you buy a ticket.

The Uffizi

MAP PAGE 38, POCKET MAP C13
Piazzale degli Uffizi. Ⓦ uffizi.it. Charge, also includes other sights.

The **Galleria degli Uffizi** is housed in what were once government offices (*uffizi*) built by Vasari for Cosimo I, which later became the home of the Medici's art collection. In the nineteenth century a large proportion of the statuary was transferred to the Bargello, while most of the antiquities went to the Museo Archeologico, leaving the Uffizi as essentially a stupendous gallery of paintings supplemented with some classical sculptures.

In the late 1990s the Uffizi began a huge renovation and expansion project, which more than doubled

Percorsi Segreti

The Palazzo Vecchio's **Percorsi Segreti** ("Secret Passageways") allows access – on guided tours only – to parts of the building that are normally off-limits, such as the Studiolo di Francesco I and the extraordinary space between the roof and ceiling of the Salone del Cinquecento. There is a small charge for tickets, in addition to the cost of entrance for the Palazzo. The hour-long tours take place most days - check online for the most up-to-date timings.

The sculpture-laden Tribuna in The Uffizi

the exhibition space by opening new suites of galleries on the first floor. There's a café and a huge bookshop too, but the so-called "Nuovo Uffizi" still seems to have fewer staff than it needs – so at any one time, you can expect to find several rooms closed. It is also useful to note that rehanging is not uncommon, so the layout might not be exactly as given below; pick up a map on your way in for the most up-to-date and accurate locations of particular artworks.

The parade of masterpieces begins immediately, with altarpieces of the *Maestà* (Madonna Enthroned) by **Duccio**, **Cimabue** and **Giotto**. Painters from fourteenth-century Siena soon follow, with several pieces by Ambrogio and Pietro Lorenzetti, and **Simone Martini**'s glorious *Annunciation*. In rooms 5–7 there's a display of paintings that mark the summit of the precious style known as International Gothic; the outstanding pieces here are **Lorenzo Monaco**'s *Coronation of the Virgin* (1415) and the *Adoration of the Magi* (1423) by **Gentile da Fabriano**.

In **Room 8**, you'll see Fra' Angelico's gorgeous *Coronation of the Virgin* and **Paolo Uccello**'s *The Battle of San Romano*, which once hung in Lorenzo il Magnifico's bedchamber. A lot of space in this room is given over to **Filippo Lippi**, whose *Madonna and Child with Two Angels* supplies one of the gallery's most popular faces: the model was Lucrezia Buti, a convent novice who became his mistress. Lucrezia puts in another appearance in Lippi's *Coronation of the Virgin*, where she's the young woman gazing out in the right foreground; Filippo himself, hand on chin, makes eye contact on the left side of the picture.

A staggering array of work by Filippo Lippi's pupil, **Botticelli**, fills the connected rooms 10–14. *The Primavera* and *The Birth of Venus* are the crowd-pullers, but don't overlook Botticelli's wonderful religious paintings, such as the *Madonna of the Magnificat* and the *Madonna of the Pomegranate*. Room 15, home to Botticelli's *Adoration of the Magi*, is dominated by the beautiful *Adoration of the Shepherds* by his

Flemish contemporary **Hugo van der Goes**.

Beyond the octagonal **Tribuna**, which houses several items from the Medici's collection of **classical sculptures**, rooms 19–23 are devoted to non-Tuscan painters of the early Italian Renaissance. Room 20 is particularly strong, with a pair of gorgeous pictures by **Antonello da Messina**, a perplexing *Sacred Allegory* by **Giovanni Bellini**, beautiful paintings by **Cima da Conegliano** and **Carpaccio**, and a stupendous array of works by **Mantegna**.

On the opposite side of the Uffizi, a room is given over to Raphael's teacher, **Perugino**, who is represented by a typically placid and contemplative *Madonna and Child with Saints* (1493), and *Pietà* (1494–95). Next comes Filippino Lippi, who shares space with **Piero di Cosimo**, creator of the bizarre *Perseus Freeing Andromeda and The Incarnation*. In this part of the Uffizi the biggest draw is the **Michelangelo** room, where the focal point is his *Doni Tondo*, the only easel painting he came close to completing. Works from various illustrious contemporaries of Michelangelo occupy the rest of the wall space.

Beyond the majestic **Niobe Room**, room 45 is currently being used as a sort of parking space for pictures that await a permanent home. Downstairs, the section devoted to **non-Italian artists** has no fewer than four Rembrandt portraits; Goya, El Greco and Chardin are just a few of the other great foreigners you'll find here. Most of this floor, however, is taken up with Italian art. **Andrea del Sarto**, **Leonardo da Vinci**, **Rosso Fiorentino** and **Pontormo** are given solo rooms, while Pontormo's protegé, **Bronzino**, gets even more space. Room 66 is packed with pictures by **Raphael**, then come **Correggio** and **Parmigianino**, followed by the Venetians: room 83 is given over to **Titian**, with eleven of his paintings on show. Works by **Salvator Rosa**, **Luca Giordano** and **Artemisia Gentileschi** make a strong impact in the last rooms, where the dominant presence is **Caravaggio**.

Armillary sphere in the Museo Galileo

Uffizi practicalities

Queues for on-the-day admission to the Uffizi in high season take hours upon hours to painstakingly inch forward, so in summer you'd be wise to pay the surcharge for booking a ticket in advance. Tickets can be reserved at the Uffizi, or at the Firenze Musei ticket booths at Orsanmichele and the Libreria My Accademia, Via Ricasoli 105r, or by calling ☎ 055 294 883 (the operators speak English). Even if you have bought an advance ticket, you should aim to get there half an hour before your allotted admission time, because the queues are often enormous.

You should also make a beeline for the first floor, which reopened in 2023 as a permanent exhibition. Here you'll find 12 pink rooms showcasing 255 self-portraits, organized chronologically. Refreshingly, an effort has been made to showcase the work of women and people of colour in addition to works by the ever-present classics, and you'll find works by Yayoi Kusama, Ai Weiwei and Hélène de Beauvoir alongside the likes of Rubens and Rembrandt.

The Museo Galileo

MAP PAGE 38, POCKET MAP C13
Piazza dei Giudici 1. ⊕ museogalileo.it.
Charge.

Long after Florence had declined from its artistic apogee, the intellectual reputation of the city was maintained by its scientists, many of them directly encouraged by the ruling Medici-Lorraine dynasty. Two of the latter, Grand Duke Ferdinando II and his brother Leopoldo, both of whom studied with Galileo, founded a scientific academy at the Pitti in 1657. Called the Accademia del Cimento (Academy of Experiment), its motto was "Try and try again." The instruments made and acquired by this academy are the core of the city's science museum, later rebranded as the **Museo Galileo**.

Some of Galileo's original instruments are on show on the first floor, such as the telescope with which he discovered the four moons of Jupiter, which he tactfully named the Medicean planets. On this floor you'll also find the museum's holy relics – bones from three of Galileo's fingers, plus a tooth. Other cases are filled with beautiful Arab astrolabes, calculating machines, early telescopes, and some delicate and ornate thermometers. The most imposing single exhibit on this floor is a massive armillary sphere made in 1593 for Ferdinando I to provide a visual proof of the supposed veracity of the earth-centred Ptolemaic system.

On the floor above there are all kinds of exquisitely manufactured scientific and mechanical equipment, several built to demonstrate the fundamental laws of physics. Dozens of clocks and timepieces are on show too, along with some spectacular electrical machines, cases of alarming surgical instruments, and anatomical wax models for teaching obstetrics.

On the ground floor, on your way out, you'll go through an interactive area that explicates the principles underlying some of the exhibits upstairs; video screens in some of the upper rooms do a similar job.

The Badìa Fiorentina

MAP PAGE 38, POCKET MAP D12
Via del Proconsolo. Free.

The Badìa Fiorentina, one of the most impressive churches in the centre of the city, was founded in 978 by Willa, widow of the Margrave of Tuscany, in honour of her husband, and it became one of the focal buildings in medieval Florence. The city's sick were treated in a hospital founded here in 1031, while the main bell marked the divisions of the working day. It was chosen as the venue for Boccaccio's celebrated lectures on Dante, which the city authorities commissioned in 1373.

The Badia's hospital owed much to Willa's son, Ugo, who further endowed his mother's foundation after a vision of hellish torments. The 1280s saw the church overhauled, and later Baroque additions smothered much of the old church, though the narrow campanile escaped unharmed. Completed around 1330, it remains a prominent feature of the Florentine skyline.

Inside the church you'll find the tomb monument to Ugo, sculpted by Mino da Fiesole between 1469 and 1481. The other outstanding work of art is Filippino Lippi's superb *Apparition of the Virgin to St Bernard* (c.1485), in which Bernard is shown in the act of writing a homily aimed at those caught between the "rocks" of tribulation and the "chains" of sin; the presence of the four monks reinforces the message that redemption lies in the contemplative life.

Nowadays the Badia belongs to the Fraternity of Jerusalem, a French monastic order founded in the 1970s, which allows tourists to peep into the church whenever a service isn't in progress. Only on Monday afternoons, however, are visitors allowed to see the upper storey of the **Chiostro degli Aranci** (Cloister of the Oranges), which is named after the citrus trees that used to be grown here. Two of its flanks are graced with an anonymous but highly distinctive fresco cycle (1436–39) on the life of St Benedict. A later panel,

showing the saint throwing himself into bushes to resist temptation, is by the young Bronzino.

The Bargello

MAP PAGE 38, POCKET MAP D12
Via del Proconsolo 4.
Ⓦ bargellomusei.beniculturali.it. Charge.

The Museo Nazionale del **Bargello** occupies the dour Palazzo del Bargello, which was built in 1255 and soon became the seat of the *Podestà*, the city's chief magistrate, and the site of the main law court. The building acquired its present name after 1574, when the Medici abolished the post of *Podestà* and the building became home to the chief of police – the *Bargello*.

You've no time to catch your breath in the Bargello: the room immediately behind the ticket office is crammed with treasures, chief of which are the work of **Michelangelo**, in whose shadow every Florentine sculptor laboured.

The tipsy, soft-bellied figure of *Bacchus* (1496–97) was his first major sculpture, carved at the age of 22, a year or so before his great *Pietà* in Rome. Michelangelo's style soon evolved into something less ostentatiously virtuosic, as is shown by the tender *Tondo Pitti* (1503–05), while the rugged expressivity of his late manner is exemplified by the square-jawed *Bust of Brutus* (c.1540), the artist's sole work of this kind. A powerful portrait sketch in stone, it's a coded celebration of anti-Medicean republicanism, carved soon after the murder of the nightmarish Duke Alessandro de' Medici.

Works by Michelangelo's followers and contemporaries are ranged in the immediate vicinity. **Benvenuto Cellini** and **Giambologna** are the best of them, and there's more Giambologna at the top of the courtyard staircase, where the first-floor loggia has been turned into a menagerie for the bronze animals and birds he made

The courtyard of the Bargello

for the Medici villa at Castello, just outside Florence.

The doorway to the right opens into the Salone del Consiglio Generale, the museum's second key room, where the presiding genius is **Donatello**, the fountainhead of Renaissance sculpture. In addition to his great statue of *St George* the room holds two figures of *David* – the later one (1430–40) was the first freestanding nude figure created since classical times. A decade later the sculptor produced the strange prancing figure known as *Amor-Atys*, which was mistaken for a genuine statue from classical antiquity – the highest compliment the artist could have wished for. Donatello was just as comfortable with portraiture as with Christian or pagan imagery, as his breathtakingly vivid terracotta *Bust of Niccolò da Uzzano* demonstrates; it may be the earliest Renaissance portrait bust. When the occasion demanded, Donatello could also produce a straightforwardly monumental piece like the nearby

Marzocco (1418–20), Florence's heraldic lion.

Donatello's master, **Ghiberti**, is represented by his relief of *Abraham's Sacrifice*, his entry in the competition to design the Baptistery doors in 1401 (see page 28), easily missed on the right-hand wall; the treatment of the theme submitted by Brunelleschi, effectively the runner-up, is hung alongside. Set around the walls of the room, a sequence of glazed terracotta Madonnas embodies **Luca della Robbia**'s sweet-natured humanism.

The rest of this floor is occupied by a superb collection of European and Islamic applied art, with dazzling specimens of work in enamel, glass, silver, majolica and ivory: among the ivory pieces from Byzantium and medieval France you'll find combs, boxes, chess pieces, and devotional panels featuring scores of figures crammed into a space the size of a paperback.

Sculpture resumes upstairs, with a room largely devoted to the della Robbia family, a prelude to the **Sala**

dei Bronzetti, Italy's best assembly of small Renaissance bronzes. Also on this floor there's another roomful of della Robbias and a splendid display of bronze medals, featuring specimens from the great pioneer of this form of portable art, Pisanello. Lastly, there's a room devoted mainly to **Renaissance portrait busts**, where the centrepiece is Verrocchio's *David*, clearly influenced by the Donatello figure downstairs. Around the walls you'll find Mino da Fiesole's busts of Giovanni de' Medici and Piero il Gottoso (the sons of Cosimo de' Medici), Antonio del Pollaiuolo's *Young Cavalier* (which is probably another Medici portrait), and a bust labelled *Ritratto d'Ignoto* (Portrait of an Unknown Man), which may in fact depict Macchiavelli. Other outstanding pieces include Francesco Laurana's *Battista Sforza*, the *Woman Holding Flowers* by Verrocchio, and the fraught marble relief in which Verrocchio portrays the death of Francesca Tornabuoni-Pitti, from whose tomb this panel was taken.

The Casa di Dante

MAP PAGE 38, POCKET MAP D11
Via Santa Margherita 1.
ⓦ museocasadidante.it. Charge.
Fraudulently marketed as Dante's house, the **Casa di Dante** is actually a medieval pastiche dating from 1910. The museum is a homage to the poet rather than a shrine: it contains nothing directly related to his life, and it's likely Dante was born not on this site but somewhere in the street that bears his name. Many editions of the *Divina Commedia* are on show, with copies of Botticelli's illustrations to the poem and a variety of displays.

Santa Margherita de' Cerchi

MAP PAGE 38, POCKET MAP D11
Via Santa Margherita. Free.
Folklore has it that Dante married his wife, Gemma Donati, in the eleventh-century church of **Santa Margherita de' Cerchi**. There's no evidence for the claim, but the building does contain tombs belonging to the Portinari, Beatrice's family; the porch also features the Donati family crest, as this was their local parish church. The church is worth a look chiefly for its altarpiece of the *Madonna and Four Saints* by Neri di Bicci.

San Martino del Vescovo

MAP PAGE 38, POCKET MAP C12–D12
Piazza San Martino.
The tiny **San Martino del Vescovo** stands on the site of an oratory that served as the Alighieris' parish church. Rebuilt in 1479, it later became the headquarters of the **Compagnia di Buonomini**, a charitable body dedicated to aiding impoverished citizens for whom begging was too demeaning. The Buonomini commissioned from Ghirlandaio's workshop a sequence of frescoes showing altruistic acts and scenes from the life of St Martin, and the result is as absorbing a record of daily life in Renaissance Florence as are the Ghirlandaio frescoes in Santa Maria Novella.

The Torre della Castagna

MAP PAGE 38, POCKET MAP D11–D12
Piazza San Martino. Free.
Opposite San Martino del Vescovo soars the thirteenth-century **Torre della Castagna**, meeting place of the city's *Priori* before they decamped to the Palazzo Vecchio. This is one of the most striking remnants of Florence's medieval townscape, when more than 150 such towers rose between the river and the Duomo, many of them over two hundred feet high. Allied clans would link their towers with **wooden catwalks**, creating a sort of upper-class promenade above the heads of the lowlier citizens. In 1250 the government of the *Primo Popolo* ordered that the towers be reduced by two-thirds of their

The Corridoio Vasariano

A door on the Uffizi's west corridor, between rooms 25 and 34, opens onto the **Corridoio Vasariano**, a passageway built by Vasari in 1565 to link the Palazzo Vecchio to the Palazzo Pitti, via the Uffizi. Winding its way down to the river, over the Ponte Vecchio, through the church of Santa Felìcita and into the Giardino di Boboli, it gives a fascinating series of clandestine views of the city. As if that weren't pleasure enough, the corridor is lined with paintings, the larger portion of which comprises a gallery of **self-portraits**, featuring such greats as Andrea del Sarto, Bronzino, Rubens, Velazquez, David, Delacroix and Ingres. However, there are plans to move the best of the paintings into the extended Uffizi galleries, and access to the corridor is erratic – various private companies offer visits, but the Uffizi sometimes opens the corridor for small-group guided tours by Uffizi staff (usually in Italian only). For the latest situation, ask at the Amici degli Uffizi office at the Uffizi or at one of the tourist offices.

height; the resulting rubble was voluminous enough to extend the city walls beyond the Arno.

Orsanmichele

MAP PAGE 38, POCKET MAP C12
Via dei Calzaiuoli.
ⓦ bargellomusei.beniculturali.it. Free.
Looming like a fortress over Via dei Calzaiuoli, the foursquare **Orsanmichele** is the oddest church in Florence – a unique hybrid of the sacred and secular, it resembles no other church in the city, and it's not even immediately apparent which of its walls is the front. It's a major monument in itself, and its exterior was once the most impressive outdoor sculpture gallery in the city. Nowadays all of the pieces outside are replicas; most of the originals are in the attached museum.

The first building here was a small oratory secreted in the vegetable garden (*orto*) of a now-vanished Benedictine monastery. A larger church stood on the site from the ninth century: San Michele ad Hortum, later San Michele in Orte – hence the compacted form of Orsanmichele. This church was replaced by a grain market in the thirteenth century, and this in turn was replaced by a loggia designed to serve as a trade hall for the *Arti Maggiori*, the Great Guilds which governed the city. Between 1367 and 1380 the loggia was walled in, after which the site was again dedicated almost exclusively to religious functions, while the two upper storeys were used as emergency grain stores. It was the guilds who paid for the sculptures, which include Ghiberti's *John the Baptist* (the earliest life-size bronze statue of the Renaissance), Verrocchio's *The Incredulity of St Thomas*, Brunelleschi's *St Peter*, and Donatello's *St George* and *St Mark*.

Inside, the centrepiece is a pavilion-sized glass and marble **tabernacle** by Orcagna, the only significant sculptural work by the artist. Decorated with lapis lazuli, stained glass and gold, it frames a Madonna painted in 1347 by Bernardo Daddi as a replacement for the miraculous image of the Virgin, which was destroyed by a fire in 1304. The brotherhood that administered Orsanmichele paid for the tabernacle from thanksgiving donations in the aftermath of

Dante

Dante Alighieri was born in 1265 into a minor noble family. He was educated at Bologna and later at Padua, where he studied philosophy and astronomy. The defining moment in his life came in 1274 when he met the 8-year-old **Beatrice Portinari**. Himself aged just nine at the time, Dante later described the encounter by quoting the words of Homer: "She appeared to be born not of mortal man but of God." Unhappily, Beatrice's family had decided their daughter was to marry someone else – Simone de' Bardi. The ceremony took place when she was 17; seven years later she was dead. Dante, for his part, had been promised – aged 12 – to Gemma Donati. The wedding took place in 1295, when the poet was 30.

In 1289 he fought for Florence against Arezzo and helped in a campaign against Pisa. Eleven years later he was dispatched to San Gimignano, where he was entrusted with the job of coaxing the town into an alliance against Pope Boniface VIII, who had designs on Tuscany. In June of the same year, he sought to settle the widening breach between the Black (anti-imperial) and White (more conciliatory) factions of Florence's ruling Guelph party. The Black Guelphs eventually emerged triumphant, and Dante's White sympathies sealed his fate. In 1302, following trumped-up charges of corruption, he was sentenced with other Whites to two years' exile. Rejecting his city of "self-made men and fast-got gain", Dante wandered between Forlì, Verona, Padua, Luni and Venice, writing much of **The Divine Comedy** as he went, before finally settling in Ravenna, where he died in 1321.

Running to more than 14,000 lines, *La Commedia* (the *Divina* was added after Dante's death) is an extraordinarily rich allegory, recounting the poet's journey through *Inferno* (Hell), *Purgatorio* (Purgatory), and *Paradiso* (Paradise), accompanied initially by the Roman poet Virgil and then by Beatrice. Each of these three realms of the dead is depicted in 33 *canti* (a "prologue" to the *Inferno* brings the total up to 100), composed in a verse scheme called *terza rima*, in which lines of eleven syllables follow the rhyme scheme aba, bcb, cdc, ded, etc. Within this framework Dante achieves an amazing variety of tone, encompassing everything from the desperate abuse of the damned to the exalted lyricism of his vision of heaven. Equally remarkable is the fact that Dante wrote his poem in the Tuscan dialect, at a time when Latin was regarded as the only language suitable for serious subjects. Before *La Commedia*, Tuscan was the language of the street; afterwards, it began to be seen as the language of all Italian people at all levels of society.

the Black Death; so many people attributed their survival to the Madonna's intervention that the money received in 1348 alone was greater than the annual tax income of the city coffers.

Upstairs, the vaulted halls of the granary house the **Museo di Orsanmichele** (free), which is entered via the footbridge from the Palazzo dell'Arte della Lana, the building opposite the church entrance. The hall itself is remarkable, and it's home to the original versions of most of the exterior statues.

Shops

Coin

MAP PAGE 38, POCKET MAP D13
Piazza del Grano 5/6. Ⓦ coin.it.

After closing its Via dei Calzaiuoli branch in 2021, Coin reopened in a new location in 2022 in a refurbished seventeenth-century building near to the exit of the Uffizi. Its six floors still focus mostly on clothes, but you'll also find jewellery, make-up and homeware here too. This new retail space also has slightly more of a focus on Florentine and Tuscan brands than its predecessor.

Spezierie Palazzo Vecchio

MAP PAGE 38, POCKET MAP C12
Via Vaccherecia 9r.
Ⓦ spezieriepalazzovecchio.it.

This celebrated old shop sells its own natural remedies and a range of unique (and not too expensive) perfumes, such as Acqua di Caterina de' Medici, which is based on a sixteenth-century recipe.

Torrini

MAP PAGE 38, POCKET MAP D12
Via della Condotta 20r.
Ⓦ torrinifotogiornalismo.it.

The *Torrini* archive, founded in 1944 by photojournalist Giulio Torrini, is a great source of unusual postcards and prints of Florence.

Gelateria

Perchè No!

MAP PAGE 38, POCKET MAP C11
Via de' Tavolini 19r.
Ⓦ facebook.com/GelateriaPercheNo.

This superb *gelateria* has been in business since the 1930s; we recommend opting for the *crema*, the chocolate or the gorgeous pistachio, all of which are mouthwateringly good. €

Cafés, bars & snacks

All'Antico Vinaio

MAP PAGE 38, POCKET MAP D13
Via dei Neri 65r.
Ⓦ allanticovinaio.com/firenze.

This place preserves the rough-and-ready atmosphere that's made it one of Florence's most popular wine bars for the past hundred years. The *focacce* are famous and the queues perpetually huge – in fact, hordes of tourists clogging up the street have started to kill the atmosphere of this spot. If you're after a *panino*, skip the queue and try '*Ino* (see page 50) just around the corner; otherwise, simple meals are served at the tables in the other branches, over the road at 74r & 76r. €

Brac

MAP PAGE 38, POCKET MAP D13
Via dei Vagellai 18r.
Ⓦ facebook.com/libreria.brac.

Sometimes clichés are clichés for a reason: *Brac* is a real hidden gem, and a particularly good find for vegetarians and vegans. It's a café-cum-restaurant-cum-art-bookshop close to the Uffizi, but blink and

Ice cream from *Perchè No!*

you'll miss it because the entrance is small and there are no signs outside. Wander through a series of rooms and outdoor courtyards to choose between a meal at the restaurant or curling up with a coffee and a book. Not to be missed. €

Cantinetta dei Verrazzano
MAP PAGE 38, POCKET MAP C11
Via de' Tavolini 18–20r.
Ⓦ bit.ly/CantinettaDV.
Owned by Castello dei Verrazzano, a major Chianti vineyard, this wood-panelled place near Orsanmichele is part-bar, part-café and part-bakery, making its own excellent pizza, *focaccia* and cakes. A perfect spot for a light lunch. €

Il Cernacchino
MAP PAGE 38, POCKET MAP C12
Via Condotta 38r.
Ⓦ facebook.com/ilcernacchiofoodwine.
Substantial and succulent sandwiches, prepared by very friendly people, just a few yards from Piazza della Signoria. The menu also features soups and pasta dishes. There are a few seats at ground level, and more upstairs. €

I Fratellini
MAP PAGE 38, POCKET MAP C12
Via dei Cimatori 38r.
Ⓦ facebook.com/ifratellini.
This minuscule stand-up bar – which attracts a melée most lunchtimes – has been in operation since the 1870s; Armando and Michele, the current proprietors, serve 29 varieties of very reasonably priced panini, as well as local wines by the glass. €

'Ino
MAP PAGE 38, POCKET MAP C13
Via de' Georgofili 3–7r. Ⓦ inofirenze.com.
Part-delicatessen and part-sandwich bar, *'Ino* serves what are possibly the most delectable panini in Florence, all made to order, using only the finest ingredients. The wine on offer is similarly fine. €

La Prosciutteria
MAP PAGE 38, POCKET MAP D13
Via dei Neri 54r. Ⓦ laprosciutteria.com.
Always packed at lunchtime and in the evening, *La Prosciutteria* is a sort of neo-*vinaio*, serving low-price but perfectly good wine, and big platters of delicious cold meats and cheese to accompany the booze. This tiny place really delivers

Rivoire

on atmosphere: expect romantic low lighting, flushed legs of ham hanging from the ceiling and dusty wine bottles lining the walls. €

Rivoire

MAP PAGE 38, POCKET MAP C12
Piazza della Signoria 5r. Ⓦ rivoire.it.
If you want to people-watch on Florence's main square, this is the place to do so, and the outside tables are invariably packed. Founded in 1872, the café started life specializing in hot chocolate, and chocolate is still its main claim to fame. Ice creams are also good, but the sandwiches and snacks are overpriced. €

Restaurants

Antico Fattore

MAP PAGE 38, POCKET MAP C13
Via Lambertesca 1–3r. Ⓦ anticofattore.it.
Simple, wholesome and delicious Tuscan dishes dominate the menu at this classic Florentine trattoria, which has barely changed its look since the 1920s. Remarkably good value, with many main courses for under €20. €€

Gustavino

MAP PAGE 38, POCKET MAP C12
Via della Condotta 37r. Ⓦ gustavino.it.
This smart restaurant-pizzeria – with a kitchen that's in full view, both from the tables and from the street – is perhaps the best place for a full meal in the immediate vicinity of Piazza della Signoria. Tuscan staples, such as *bistecca*, feature prominently on the menu, as well as a fine selection of wines. €€

Ora d'Aria

MAP PAGE 38, POCKET MAP C13
Via dei Georgofili 11r.
Ⓦ oradariaristorante.com.
Marco Stabile, the boss of *Ora d'Aria*, has established a reputation as one of the city's best restaurateurs, thanks to menus that offer a high-quality mix of the traditional and the innovative. The various tasting menus are expensive but still very good value for such exceptional cooking; and there's an extraordinary 11-part tasting menu for those really looking to push the boat out. The bright and cool setting is the very opposite of the faux-rustic style that you often find elsewhere in Florence. €€€

Vini e Vecchi Sapori

MAP PAGE 38, POCKET MAP D12
Via dei Magazzini 3r. Ⓦ bit.ly/ViniEVecchi,
Just off the piazza, this tiny family-run trattoria is always packed – hardly surprising, as it offers solid traditional Florentine food at much lower prices than its high-toned neighbours. €€

Yellow Bar

MAP PAGE 38, POCKET MAP D11
Via del Proconsolo 39r. ☎ 055 211 766.
This place looks like a fast-food joint, but the queues of Florentines waiting for a table give you a clue that these first impressions are misleading. Inside, the convivial atmosphere in the large dining room is matched by superlative pan-Italian food (including excellent pizzas) in large portions at very reasonable prices. When the main dining room is busy you can often get a table in the rooms downstairs. €€

Club

Blob Club

MAP PAGE 38, POCKET MAP D13
Via Vinegia 21r. Ⓦ bit.ly/BlobClub.
A favourite with Florentine students, possibly on account of free admission, the 6–9pm happy hour and the fact that it stays open until the wee hours at weekends. There's seating upstairs, as well as table football, and a bar and tiny dancefloor downstairs, but don't expect to do much dancing – later on, especially on weekend nights, *Blob* gets packed with a very happy and very drunken crowd.

West of the centre

Despite the urban improvement schemes of the nineteenth century and the damage inflicted during World War II, several of the streets immediately to the west of Piazza della Signoria retain their medieval character: an amble along Via Porta Rossa, Via delle Terme and Borgo Santi Apostoli will give you some idea of the feel of Florence in the Middle Ages, when every big house was an urban fortress. The best-preserved of these medieval redoubts is the Palazzo Davanzati, whose interior looks little different from the way it did six hundred years ago. The exquisite ancient church of Santi Apostoli is nearby, as is the church of Santa Trìnita, which is home to an outstanding fresco cycle by Domenico Ghirlandaio. Beyond the glitzy Via de' Tornabuoni – the city's priciest slice of retail real estate – you'll find Ognissanti, which also has some outstanding paintings, but the major monument in this area is the fresco-filled church of Santa Maria Novella, which stands opposite the train station.

The Mercato Nuovo

MAP PAGE 54, POCKET MAP B12
Piazza di Mercato Nuovo.

The **Mercato Nuovo**, or Mercato del Porcellino, has been the site of a market since the eleventh century, though the present loggia dates from the sixteenth. Having forked out their euros at the souvenir stalls, most people join the small group that's invariably gathered round the bronze boar known as *Il Porcellino*: you're supposed to earn good luck by getting a coin to fall from the animal's mouth through the grille below his head – and by touching his snout, which has been rubbed golden by millions of hands.

Palazzo Davanzati

MAP PAGE 54, POCKET MAP B12
Via Porta Rossa 13. ⓦ bargellomusei.
beniculturali.it. Charge, joint ticket with other sights available.

Virtually every room of the fourteenth-century **Palazzo**

Davanzati is furnished and decorated in medieval style, using genuine artefacts gathered from a variety of sources.

Merchants' houses in that period would typically have had elaborately **painted walls** in the main rooms, and the Palazzo Davanzati preserves some fine examples of such decor – especially in the dining room. Before the development of systems of credit, wealth had to be sunk into assets such as the tapestries, ceramics, sculpture and lacework that alleviate the austerity of many of these rooms; any surplus cash would have been locked away in a strongbox like the extraordinary example in the **Sala Piccola**. There's also a fine collection of *cassoni*, the painted chests in which the wife's dowry would be stored.

Plushest of the rooms is the first-floor bedroom, but the spot where the occupants would have been likeliest to linger is the

kitchen. Located on the top floor to minimize the damage that might be caused by the outbreak of a fire, it would have been the warmest room in the house. A load of ancient utensils are on show here, and set into one wall there is the most civilized of amenities, a service shaft connecting the kitchen to all floors of the building. The leaded glass would have been considered a marvel at a time when many windows were covered with turpentine-soaked rags stretched across frames to repel rainwater.

Santi Apostoli

MAP PAGE 54, POCKET MAP B12–B13
Piazza del Limbo. Ⓦ santiapostoli.com.
Free.

Legend has it that the church of **Santi Apostoli** was founded by Charlemagne; it's not quite that ancient, but certainly pre-dates the end of the first millennium. Side chapels were added in the fifteenth and sixteenth centuries, yet the building still has an austere beauty quite unlike any other church in the city centre, with its expanses of bare stone wall and columns of green Prato marble.

The chief treasures of Santi Apostoli are some stone fragments from the Holy Sepulchre in Jerusalem, which on Holy Saturday are used to spark the flame that ignites the "dove" which in turn sets off the fireworks in front of the Duomo.

Santa Trìnita

MAP PAGE 54, POCKET MAP A12
Free.

Santa Trìnita was founded in 1092 by a Florentine nobleman called **Giovanni Gualberto**, scenes from whose life are illustrated in the frescoes in the fourth chapel of the left aisle. One Good Friday, so the story goes, Gualberto set off intent on avenging the murder of his brother. On finding the murderer he decided to spare his life – it was Good Friday – and proceeded to San Miniato (see page 102), where a crucifix is said to have bowed its head to honour his act of mercy. Giovanni went on to become a Benedictine monk and founded the reforming Vallombrosan order and – notwithstanding the mayhem

Santi Apostoli

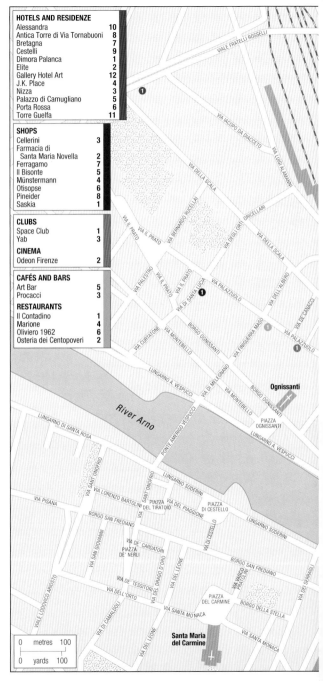

HOTELS AND RESIDENZE

Alessandra	10
Antica Torre di Via Tornabuoni	8
Bretagna	7
Cestelli	9
Dimora Palanca	1
Elite	2
Gallery Hotel Art	12
J.K. Place	4
Nizza	3
Palazzo di Camugliano	5
Porta Rossa	6
Torre Guelfa	11

SHOPS

Cellerini	3
Farmacia di Santa Maria Novella	2
Ferragamo	7
Il Bisonte	5
Münstermann	4
Otisopse	6
Pineider	8
Saskia	1

CLUBS

Space Club	1
Yab	3

CINEMA

Odeon Firenze	2

CAFÉS AND BARS

Art Bar	5
Procacci	3

RESTAURANTS

Il Contadino	1
Marione	4
Oliviero 1962	6
Osteria dei Centopoveri	2

West of the centre

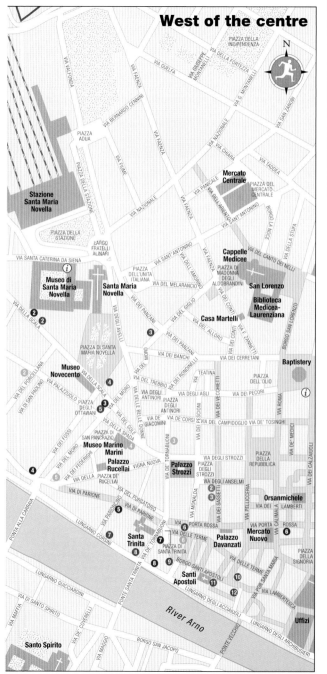

created on Florence's streets by his militant supporters – was eventually canonized.

The church was rebuilt between about 1300 and 1330, and piecemeal additions over the years have lent it a pleasantly hybrid air: the largely Gothic interior contrasts with the Mannerist facade, itself at odds with the Romanesque front wall of the interior. The fame of the building is due chiefly to Ghirlandaio's **frescoes** (1483–86) of scenes from the life of St Francis, in the Cappella Sassetti.

Commissioned by Francesco Sassetti, a friend of Lorenzo the Magnificent, these scenes were intended, in part, to eclipse the chapel in Santa Maria Novella sponsored by Sassetti's rival, Giovanni Tornabuoni, which was also painted by Ghirlandaio. St Francis, floating in the sky, is shown bringing a child back to life in Piazza Santa Trìnita, with the church in the background. (Opposite the church you can see the child plummeting to his temporary death.) Above this scene, *St Francis Receiving the Rule* sets the action in Piazza della Signoria

Ponte Santa Trìnita

and features (right foreground) a portrait of Sassetti between his son, Federigo, and Lorenzo il Magnifico (Sassetti was general manager of the Medici bank). On the steps below them are the humanist Poliziano and three of his pupils, Lorenzo's sons; the blond boy at the back of the line is Giovanni, the future Pope Leo X. Ghirlandaio has depicted himself in the lower scene, with his hand on his hip, and is also present in the chapel's altarpiece, the *Adoration of the Shepherds* (1485) – he's the shepherd pointing to the Child and, by way of self-identification, to the garland (*ghirlanda*). The figures of the donors – Sassetti and his wife, Nera Corsi – kneel to either side; they are buried in Giuliano da Sangallo's black tombs under the side arches.

Displayed in the neighbouring Cappella Doni is the miraculous crucifix that bowed its head to Gualberto. The third of the church's major works, a powerful composition by Luca della Robbia – the tomb of Benozzo Federighi, bishop of Fiesole – occupies the left wall of the Cappella Scali, the farthest chapel.

Ponte Santa Trìnita

MAP PAGE 54, POCKET MAP A12–A13

The sleek **Ponte Santa Trìnita** was built on Cosimo I's orders after its predecessor was demolished in a flood. The roads on both banks were raised and widened to accentuate the dramatic potential of the new link between the city centre and the Oltrarno, but what makes this the classiest bridge in Florence is the sensuous **curve** of its arches, a curve so shallow that engineers have been baffled as to how the bridge bears up under the strain. Ostensibly the design was devised by **Ammannati**, one of the Medici's favourite artists, but the curves so closely resemble the arc of Michelangelo's Medici tombs that it's likely the credit belongs to him.

The Paterenes and St Peter Martyr

In the twelfth century, Florence became the crucible of one of the reforming **religious movements** that periodically cropped up in medieval Europe. The Paterenes were convinced that everything worldly was touched by the Devil. Accordingly they despised the papacy for its claims to temporal power, and their campaign against the financial and moral corruption of the Catholic Church inevitably brought them into conflict with Rome. The displeasure of the Vatican found its means of expression in the Dominican known as St Peter Martyr. Operating from Santa Maria Novella, this papal inquisitor headed a couple of anti-Paterene fraternities, which were in effect his private army. In 1244 he led them into battle across Piazza Santa Maria Novella, where they massacred hundreds of the theological enemy. The carnage is commemorated by the Croce al Trebbio in Via delle Belle Donne, off the eastern side of the piazza.

After this, the Dominicans turned to less militant work, founding the charitable organization called the **Misericordia**, which is still in existence today. In 1252 Peter was knifed to death, supposedly by a pair of Paterene heretics; legend relates that the dying man managed to write out the Credo with his own blood before expiring – an incident depicted in the frescoes in Santa Maria Novella's Cappellone degli Spagnoli. Within a year he'd been made a saint.

In 1944 the Nazis blew the bridge to smithereens and seven years later it was decided to rebuild it using as much of the original material as could be dredged from the Arno. To ensure maximum authenticity, all the new stone that was needed was quarried from the Bóboli gardens, where the stone for Ammannati's bridge had been cut. Twelve years after the war ended, the reconstructed bridge was completed.

Via de' Tornabuoni

MAP PAGE 54, POCKET MAP A12

The shops of **Via de' Tornabuoni** are effectively out of bounds to those who don't travel first class. Versace, Ferragamo, Prada, Cavalli, Gucci and Armani have their outlets here: indeed, in recent years they have come to monopolize the street (and some of its tributaries), to the dismay of many, who see further evidence of the loss of Florentine identity in the eviction of local institutions such as the Seeber bookshop, the Farmacia Inglese and the *Giacosa* café.

Palazzo Strozzi

MAP PAGE 54, POCKET MAP A11

Piazza degli Strozzi. ⓦ palazzostrozzi.org. Conspicuous wealth is nothing new on Via de' Tornabuoni. Looming above everything is the vast **Palazzo Strozzi**, the largest and most intimidating of all Florentine Renaissance palaces, with windows as big as gateways and embossed with lumps of stone the size of boulders. Designed by Giuliano da Sangallo, it was begun by the banker Filippo Strozzi, a figure so powerful that he was once described as "the first man of Italy", and whose family were ringleaders of the anti-Medici faction in Florence. He bought and demolished a dozen town houses to make space for this strongbox in stone, and its construction lasted from 1489 to 1536. Not until the 1930s did the Strozzi family relinquish ownership of the building, which is now administered by the Fondazione Palazzo Strozzi, under whose administration the building has become a venue for outstanding art exhibitions; it has a nice café too.

Palazzo Rucellai

MAP PAGE 54, POCKET MAP C5
Via della Vigna Nuova 18.
In the 1440s Giovanni Rucellai, one of the richest businessmen in the city (and an esteemed scholar too), decided to commission a new house from **Leon Battista Alberti**, whose accomplishments as architect, mathematician, linguist and theorist of the arts prompted a contemporary to exclaim, "Where shall I put Battista Alberti: in what category of learned men shall I place him?" The resultant **Palazzo Rucellai**, two minutes' walk from the Strozzi house at Via della Vigna Nuova 18, was the first palace in Florence to follow the rules of classical architecture; its tiers of pilasters, incised into smooth blocks of stone, evoke the exterior wall of the Colosseum.

Palazzo Rucellai

Alberti later produced another, equally elegant design for the same patron – the front of the church of Santa Maria Novella. In contrast to the feud between the Medici and the Strozzi, the Rucellai were on the closest terms with the city's *de facto* royal family: the **Loggia dei Rucellai**, across the street (now a shop), was in all likelihood built for the wedding of Giovanni's son to the granddaughter of Cosimo il Vecchio, and the frieze on the Palazzo Rucellai features the heraldic devices of the two families, the Medici emblem alongside the Rucellai sail.

The Museo Marino Marini and Cappella Rucellai

MAP PAGE 54, POCKET MAP A11
Piazza San Pancrazio.
ⓦ **museomarinomarini.it. Charge.**
Round the corner from the Palazzo Rucellai stands the ex-church of San Pancrazio, deconsecrated by Napoleon, then successively the offices of the state lottery, the magistrates' court, a tobacco factory and an arsenal. It's now the **Museo Marino Marini**, a superbly designed space which holds some two hundred works that were left to the city in Marini's will. Born in Pistoia in 1901, Marini trained at the Accademia and devoted most of his subsequent career to sculpture, developing a distinctive style in which the mythical and the modern were powerfully fused. His equestrian figures are his best-known works, and variations of the theme make a strong showing here, alongside some potent nudes.

Once part of San Pancrazio church and now entered via the museum, the **Cappella Rucellai**, which was redesigned by Alberti, houses the marble-clad **Tempietto dello Santo Sepolcro**, the most exquisite of his architectural creations. Its form is derived from ancient Christian chapels that were themselves built in imitation of the Holy Sepulchre in Jerusalem, and its decoration is derived from Romanesque Tuscan churches such as San Miniato (see page 102). Commissioned by Giovanni Rucellai as his own funerary monument, the Tempietto was completed in 1467, more than a decade before Giovanni's death. Visits to the chapel have to be booked in advance at the museum.

Stazione Santa Maria Novella

MAP PAGE 54, POCKET MAP C3–C4

Most visitors barely spare a glance for Santa Maria Novella train **station**, but it's a superb building. It was in 1933 that its principal architect, Giovanni Michelucci (1891–1990), won the competition to design a new main rail terminal for the city, and its planning is so impeccably rational that it proved to be adequate for the city's needs until the start of this century.

Santa Maria Novella

MAP PAGE 54, POCKET MAP C4

Piazza Santa Maria Novella ⓦ smn.it. Charge, also includes the museum.

The graceful **church** of Santa Maria Novella was the Florentine base of the Dominican order, the vigilantes of thirteenth-century Catholicism. A more humble church, Santa Maria delle Vigne, which had existed here since the eleventh century, was handed to the Dominicans in 1221; they then set about altering the place to their taste. By 1360 the interior was finished, but only the Romanesque lower part of the **facade** had been completed. This state of affairs lasted until 1456, when Giovanni Rucellai paid for Alberti to design a classical upper storey that would blend with the older section while improving the facade's proportions. The sponsor's name is picked out across the facade in Roman capitals, while the Rucellai family

Stazione Santa Maria Novella

emblem, the billowing sail of Fortune, runs as a motif through the central frieze.

Santa Maria Novella's **interior**, which was designed to enable preachers to address their sermons to as large a congregation as possible, is adorned with a ground-breaking painting by Masaccio, a crucifix by Giotto and no fewer than three major fresco cycles. **Masaccio**'s extraordinary 1427 depiction of the **Trinity**, painted on the wall of the left aisle, was one of the earliest works in which the rules of perspective and classical proportion were rigorously employed, and Florentines queued to view the illusion on its unveiling, stunned by a painting which appeared to create three-dimensional space on a solid wall.

Giotto's crucifix, a radically naturalistic and probably very early work (c.1288–90), hangs in what is thought to be its intended position, poised dramatically over the centre of the nave. Hitherto, it had been hidden away in the sacristy, veiled by a layer of dirt so thick that many scholars refused to recognize it as the work of the master; the attribution is still disputed by some.

The chapel to the right of the chancel is covered with a fabulous cycle of frescoes commissioned in 1489 from **Filippino Lippi** by the banker Filippo Strozzi. Illustrating the life of Strozzi's namesake, St Philip the Apostle, the paintings were commenced after Filippino had spent some time in Rome, and the work he carried out on his return displays an archeologist's obsession with ancient Roman culture. Behind the altar is Strozzi's tomb (1491–95), beautifully carved by Benedetto da Maiano.

As a chronicle of fifteenth-century life in Florence, no series of frescoes is more fascinating than **Domenico Ghirlandaio**'s pictures around the chancel and high altar. The artist's masterpiece, the pictures were commissioned by Giovanni Tornabuoni, a banker and uncle of Lorenzo de' Medici (Lorenzo the Magnificent), which explains why certain illustrious ladies of the Tornabuoni family are present at the births of both John the Baptist and the Virgin. These frescoes are a proud celebration of Florence at its zenith – indeed, one of the frescoes includes a Latin inscription which reads: "The year 1490, when the most beautiful city renowned for abundance, victories, arts and noble buildings profoundly enjoyed salubrity and peace." Ghirlandaio himself features in the scene in which Joachim, the Virgin's father, is chased from the temple because he has been unable to have children – the painter is the figure in the right-hand group with hand on hip.

The church's third great fresco cycle is in the **Cappella Strozzi**, which lies above the level of the rest of the church at the end of the left transept. Commissioned in 1350 as an expiation of the sin of usury by Tommaso Strozzi, an ancestor of Filippo Strozzi, the pictures are the masterpiece of Nardo di Cione, brother of the better-known Orcagna (Andrea di Cione), who painted the chapel's magnificent high altarpiece, *Christ Presenting the Keys to St Peter and the Book of Wisdom to Thomas Aquinas* (1357). Behind the altar, the central fresco depicts the *Last Judgement*, with Dante featured as one of the saved (in white, third from the left, second row from the top). So, too, are Tommaso Strozzi and his wife, shown being led by St Michael into paradise, with an angel helping the righteous up through a trapdoor; on the right of the altar, a devil forks the damned down into hell. The theme of judgement is continued in the fresco of Dante's *Inferno* on the right wall, faced by a thronged *Paradiso*.

The adjacent chapel, the Cappella Gondi, contains a crucifix carved by Brunelleschi, supposedly as a riposte to the uncouthness of Donatello's crucifix in Santa Croce.

The Museo di Santa Maria Novella

MAP PAGE 54, POCKET MAP C4
Piazza Santa Maria Novella, entered via the church or at Piazza della Stazione 4. Ⓦ smn.it. Charge, also includes the church of Santa Maria Novella.

Remarkable paintings are housed in the spacious Romanesque conventual buildings of Santa Maria Novella, now home to the **Museo di Santa Maria Novella**. The main cloister, the **Chiostro Verde**, dates from the fourteenth century and features frescoes of *Stories from Genesis* (1425–30) executed by Paolo Uccello and his workshop. The cloister takes its name from the green base *terra verde* pigment they used, and which now gives the paintings a spectral undertone. Best preserved of the frescoes is *The Flood*, a windswept scene rendered almost unintelligible by the telescoping perspective and the double appearance of the Ark (before and after the flood), whose flanks form a receding corridor in the centre of the picture.

Off the cloister opens the **Cappellone degli Spagnoli**, or Spanish Chapel, which received its present name after Eleonora di Toledo, wife of Cosimo I, reserved it for the use of her Spanish entourage. Presumably she derived much inspiration from its majestic fresco cycle (1367–69) by Andrea di Firenze, an extended depiction of the triumph of the Catholic Church that was described by Ruskin as "the most noble piece of pictorial philosophy in Italy". Virtually every patch of the walls is covered with frescoes, whose theme is the role of the Dominicans in the battle against heresy and in the salvation of Christian souls. Most spectacular is the right wall, depicting *The Triumph of the Church*. The Dominicans are of course prominent among the ranks of figures representing religious orders: note St Dominic, the order's founder, unleashing the "hounds of the lord", or *Domini Canes*, a pun on the Dominicans' name.

The decoration of the Chiostrino dei Morti, the oldest part of the complex, has not aged so robustly, but the Chiostro Grande, the largest cloister in Florence, has extensive sixteenth- and seventeenth-century frescoes of scenes from the life of Christ and St Dominic, while traces of fourteenth-century decoration can be seen in the old dormitory. On the upper floor, the chapel has a gorgeous fresco of St Veronica, painted by the young Pontormo in 1515.

Museo Novecento

MAP PAGE 54, POCKET MAP C5
Piazza Santa Maria Novella 14ar
W museonovecento.it. Charge.

The colonnaded building facing Santa Maria Novella across the piazza was formerly a hospital, which was founded back in the thirteenth century and rebuilt in the second half of the fifteenth, probably to a design by Michelozzo. Soon after its completion, Andrea della Robbia added the attractive terracotta

Cappellone degli Spagnoli

Chiostro Verde, Santa Maria Novella

medallions to the loggia. In the 1780s it became a crafts school for poor unmarried women, a function it retained until the twentieth century, when it was converted into a school for children. Now, having been restored, it's home to Florence's newest civic museum, the **Museo Novecento**, featuring some of the heavyweights of Italian twentieth-century art, such as Giorgio Morandi, Giorgio de Chirico, Lucio Fontana and Emilio Vedova.

Ognissanti

MAP PAGE 54, POCKET MAP B5
Borgo Ognissanti. Free.

In medieval times one of the main areas of cloth production – the mainstay of the Florentine economy – was in the west of the city. San Salvatore in **Ognissanti**, the main church of this quarter, stands on a piazza that might be taken as a symbol of the state of the present-day Florentine economy, dominated as it is by two of Florence's plushest hotels. The church was founded in 1256 by the Umiliati, a Benedictine order

from Lombardy who specialized in weaving woollen cloth; in 1561 the Franciscans took over the church, the new tenure being marked by a Baroque overhaul which spared only the medieval campanile.

The young face squeezed between the Madonna and the dark-cloaked man in Ghirlandaio's *Madonna della Misericordia* (1473), over the second altar on the right, is said to be that of Amerigo Vespucci (1451–1512), an agent for the Medici in Seville, whose two voyages in 1499 and 1501 would lend his name to a continent. The altar was paid for by the Vespucci, a family of silk merchants from the Ognissanti district, which is why other members of the clan appear beneath the Madonna's cloak. Among them is Simonetta Vespucci (at the Virgin's left hand), the mistress of Giuliano de' Medici – she is said to have been the model for the face of Botticelli's Venus. The idea may not be so far-fetched, for Botticelli was born in the Ognissanti parish and lived locally, and the Vespucci and Filipepi families were on good terms. Botticelli is buried in the church, beneath a round tomb slab in the south transept (the slab bears his baptismal name, Sandro Filipepi), and his small fresco of *St Augustine's Vision of St Jerome* (1480) hangs on the same wall as the Madonna, between the third and fourth altars. Facing it is Ghirlandaio's more earthbound *St Jerome*, also painted in 1480; in the same year Ghirlandaio painted the *Last Supper* that covers one wall of the refectory, reached through the cloister entered to the left of the church. And don't miss the dazzling **Crucifix** that hangs in the left transept of Ognissanti: it emerged from a seven-year restoration in 2010, and during cleaning it was established by infrared and X-ray analysis that it's almost certainly by Giotto.

Shops

Il Bisonte

MAP PAGE 54, POCKET MAP A12
Via del Parione 31–33r. ⓦ ilbisonte.com.
Beautiful and robust bags, briefcases and accessories, many of them made from *vacchetta*, a soft cowhide that ages very nicely.

Cellerini

MAP PAGE 54, POCKET MAP C5
Via del Sole 9. ⓦ cellerini.it.
Bags, bags and more bags, from the city's premier exponents of the craft. Their handiwork is elegant, durable and accordingly costly.

Farmacia di Santa Maria Novella

MAP PAGE 54, POCKET MAP C4
Via della Scala 16. ⓦ smnovella.it.
Occupying the pharmacy of the Santa Maria Novella monastery, this sixteenth-century shop was founded by Dominican monks as an outlet for their potions, ointments and herbal remedies. Many of these are still available,
including distillations of flowers, together with face-creams and shampoos.

Ferragamo

MAP PAGE 54, POCKET MAP A12
Via de' Tornabuoni 14r.
ⓦ salvatoreferragamo.it.
Established by Salvatore Ferragamo, once the most famous shoemaker in the world, Ferragamo now produces ready-to-wear clothing too, but the company's reputation still rests on its beautiful shoes. The shop is unbelievably grandiose, and has a museum in the basement, featuring shoes that Salvatore made for Marilyn Monroe.

Münstermann

MAP PAGE 54, POCKET MAP C5
Piazza Goldoni 2r. ⓦ munstermann.it.
Münstermann has been producing its own soaps and perfumes since the end of the nineteenth century, and the recipes it uses today are virtually unchanged. Perfect if you want something a little different from the usual duty-free offerings.

Farmacia di Santa Maria Novella

Otisopse

MAP PAGE 54, POCKET MAP C12
Via Porta Rossa 13r. ⓦ otisopse.com.

Florentine footwear is of famously high quality, but can be rather staid. Otisopse, founded in Naples in 1929, goes instead for the cheap and cheerful approach – a pair of their pink desert boots or purple moccasins will cost you around €50. There are two other branches, both in Oltrarno: Via Guiccardini 2r and Piazza Nazario Sauro 7r.

Pineider

MAP PAGE 54, POCKET MAP A12
Lungarno degli Acciaiuoli 72r.
ⓦ pineider.com.

Pineider sells briefcases, picture frames and other accessories for the home and office, but its reputation rests on its colour-coordinated calling cards, handmade papers and envelopes – as used by Napoleon, Stendhal, Byron and Shelley, to name just a few of its famed customers.

Saskia

MAP PAGE 54, POCKET MAP B4
Via di Santa Lucia 24r.
ⓦ saskiascarpesumisura.com.

Berlin-born Saskia Wittmer trained at John Lobb in London and with Stefano Bemer in Florence, before setting up her own workshop near Ognissanti. Producing exquisite made-to-measure shoes in classic designs, she specializes in men's footwear, but makes a few designs for women too. Such quality does not come cheap, of course – we're talking upwards of €2000 for a pair.

Cafés & bars

Art Bar

MAP PAGE 54, POCKET MAP C5
Via del Moro 4r. ☎ 055 287 661.

A fine little bar near Piazza di Carlo Goldoni. The interior looks like an antique shop, while the club-like atmosphere attracts a smart crowd. Busiest at happy hour (6.30–9pm),

Cocktail at *Art Bar*

when the imaginative cocktails are in heavy demand. €

Procacci

MAP PAGE 54, POCKET MAP A11
Via de' Tornabuoni 64r. Ⓦ procacci1885.it.
Serving just wine and cold drinks, this famous café's reputation comes from the extraordinary, tiny and delicious *tartufati* (truffle-butter brioche). In fact, try anything on the menu that comes with truffle – it's a solid bet! €€

Restaurants

Il Contadino

MAP PAGE 54, POCKET MAP B4
Via Palazzuolo 69–71r. Ⓦ facebook.com/trattoriailcontadinofirenze.
This no-frills trattoria has been popular since it opened for business in the 1970s, and it hasn't changed its style much since then, with its monochrome tiled dining room and refectory-like seating. Service is fast and friendly, and the food is delicious and very cheap – you can easily get wine and two courses for less than €20. No reservations. €

Marione

MAP PAGE 54, POCKET MAP A11
Via della Spada 27r. Ⓦ trattoriamarione.it.
This simple old trattoria is a reliable stand-by. It's not the most refined cooking in Florence and the ambience is brisk rather than homely, but with solid Tuscan main courses including *ribollita* and *bistecca* for under €15 you can't really complain. €

Oliviero 1962

MAP PAGE 54, POCKET MAP A12
Via delle Terme 52r.
Ⓦ ristoranteoliviero.com.
Soon after opening in 1962, *Oliviero* established itself as one of the city's finest and most glamorous restaurants. Charming and romantic, you can expect gorgeous gourmet dishes and friendly, fast service. €€€

Osteria dei Centopoveri

MAP PAGE 54, POCKET MAP C5
Via Palazzuolo 31r & 41r. Ⓦ centopoveri.it.
This very popular *osteria* offers more fish than is customary on a generally meat-oriented Tuscan menu, and has some excellent set menus (both fish and meat). Established in the 1990s, the operation has expanded in recent years, and pizzas are served at the newer branch, at 41r. €€

Clubs

Space Club

MAP PAGE 54, POCKET MAP B4
Via Palazzuolo 37.
Ⓦ instagram.com/spaceclubfirenze.
Having operated for years under the name *Space Electronic*, the refurbished *Space Club* is still the archetypal big Continental disco, with Florence's biggest dancefloor. There's a cloakroom service, which you should take advantage of because it gets very hot inside - make sure you take a photo of your ticket just in case you happen to lose it in the night.

Yab

MAP PAGE 54, POCKET MAP B12
Via de' Sassetti 5r. Ⓦ yab.it.
This basement club-bar-restaurant is known throughout the country for Monday's "Yabsmoove" – Italy's longest-running hip-hop night. If hip-hop isn't your thing, there are other themed nights throughout the week.

Cinema

Odeon Firenze

MAP PAGE 54, POCKET MAP B11
Piazza Strozzi 2. Ⓦ odeonfirenze.com.
Mainstream films are screened in their original language (with Italian subtitles) at this air-conditioned cinema almost every day.
Also showing art-house and independent movies.

North of the centre

The San Lorenzo district, to the northwest of the Duomo, is the city's main market area, with scores of clothing and accessories stalls encircling a vast food hall. Racks of T-shirts, leather jackets and belts fill the road beside the church of San Lorenzo, a building of major importance, to which is attached another of the city's major draws, the Cappelle Medicee (Medici Chapels). While some of the most prominent members of the Medici family are buried in the main part of San Lorenzo, dozens of lesser lights are interred in these chapels, with two of them being celebrated by some of Michelangelo's finest sculptures. The Medici also account for the area's other major sight, the Palazzo Medici-Riccardi, to the north of which lies the Museo di San Marco, replete with paintings by Fra' Angelico. A brief walk from San Marco brings you to the Accademia, famous above all for Michelangelo's David. A short distance to the east is the graceful Piazza Santissima Annunziata, site of Brunelleschi's Spedale degli Innocenti, the superb church of Santissima Annunziata and the Museo Archeologico.

San Lorenzo

MAP PAGE 68, POCKET MAP D4
Piazza San Lorenzo.
Ⓦ operamedicealaurenziana.org. Charge.
Founded in 393, **San Lorenzo** has a claim to be the oldest church in Florence, and for some three hundred years it was the city's cathedral. By 1060 a sizeable Romanesque church had been built on the site, a building which in time became the Medici's parish church. In 1419 Giovanni di Bicci de' Medici, founder of the Medici fortune, offered to finance a new church, designed by **Brunelleschi**, but construction was hampered by financial problems. Giovanni's son, Cosimo de' Medici, eventually saved the day, but his largesse was not sufficient to provide the church with a facade, a feature it still lacks.

What strikes you on stepping **inside the church** is the cool rationality of Brunelleschi's design, an instantly calming contrast to the hubbub outside. The first work of art to catch your attention, in the second chapel on the right, is Rosso Fiorentino's *Marriage of the Virgin* (1523), with its golden-haired and youthful Joseph. There's another arresting painting at the top of the left aisle – Bronzino's enormous fresco of *The Martyrdom of St Lawrence* (1569) – but it seems a shallow piece of work alongside the nearby bronze pulpits by Donatello. Clad with reliefs depicting scenes preceding and following the Crucifixion, these are the artist's last works (begun c.1460) and were completed by his pupils as increasing paralysis limited their master's ability to model in wax. Jagged and discomforting, charged with more energy than the space can contain, these panels are more like virtuoso sketches in bronze than conventional reliefs. Donatello is buried in the nave of the church, next to his patron, Cosimo de' Medici, and commemorated by a memorial in the chapel in the north transept, close to Filippo Lippi's altarpiece of the *Annunciation*. Cosimo's own tomb, in the centre of the church, bears the inscription "Pater Patriae" (Father of the Fatherland) – a title once borne by Roman emperors.

Four other eminent Medici lie buried in the **Sagrestia Vecchia**, one of Brunelleschi's earliest projects (1421–26), and the only one completed in his lifetime. The space was commissioned by Giovanni Bicci de' Medici as a private chapel; on his death, Giovanni was buried beneath the massive marble slab at the centre of the chapel, with his wife, Piccarda. Another tomb, on the left as you enter, is the resting place of Giovanni's grandsons, Giovanni and Piero de' Medici. Donatello created the cherub-filled frieze and the eight tondi above it, depicting the Four Evangelists and a quartet of scenes from the life of St John; he was also responsible for the two bronze doors, showing pairs of disputatious martyrs (the left door), and the Apostles and Fathers of the Church (the right).

The Biblioteca Medicea-Laurenziana

MAP PAGE 68, POCKET MAP D4
Piazza San Lorenzo.
Ⓦ operamedicealaurenziana.org. Charge.
A gateway to the left of San Lorenzo leads to the **Biblioteca Medicea-Laurenziana**. Wishing to create a suitably grandiose home for the family's precious manuscripts, Pope Clement VII – Lorenzo's nephew – asked Michelangelo to design a new library in 1524. The **Ricetto**, or vestibule, of the building he eventually came up with (more than thirty years later) is a showpiece of Mannerist architecture, delighting in

paradoxical display: brackets that support nothing, columns that sink into the walls, and a flight of steps so large that it almost fills the room.

In the reading room, too, almost everything is the work of Michelangelo. Exhibitions in the connecting rooms draw on the 15,000-piece Medici collection, which includes manuscripts as diverse as a fifth-century copy of Virgil – the collection's oldest item – and a treatise on architecture by Leonardo.

The Cappelle Medicee

MAP PAGE 68, POCKET MAP D4
Piazza Madonna degli Aldobrandini.
Ⓦ bargellomusei.beniculturali.it. Charge.
Michelangelo's most celebrated contribution to the San Lorenzo complex forms part of the **Cappelle Medicee**, which are entered from Piazza Madonna degli Aldobrandini, at the back of the church.

After passing through the crypt, where almost fifty lesser Medici are buried, you climb up to the Cappella dei Principi (Chapel of the Princes), an oppressively

Piazza San Lorenzo

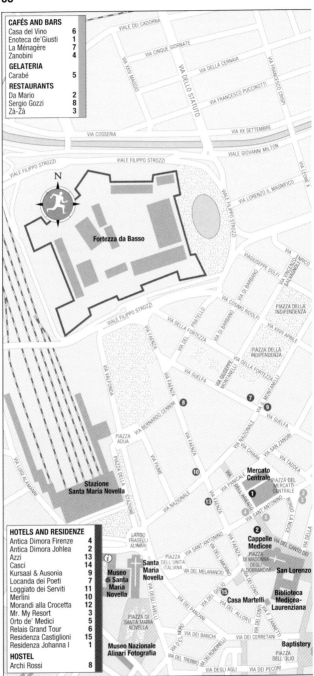

CAFÉS AND BARS

Casa del Vino	6
Enoteca de'Giusti	1
La Ménagère	7
Zanobini	4

GELATERIA

Carabé	5

RESTAURANTS

Da Mario	2
Sergio Gozzi	8
Zà-Zà	3

HOTELS AND RESIDENZE

Antica Dimora Firenze	4
Antica Dimora Johlea	2
Azzi	13
Casci	14
Kursaal & Ausonia	9
Locanda dei Poeti	7
Loggiato dei Serviti	11
Merlini	10
Morandi alla Crocetta	12
Mr. My Resort	3
Orto de' Medici	5
Relais Grand Tour	6
Residenza Castiglioni	15
Residenza Johanna I	1

HOSTEL

Archi Rossi	8

North of the centre

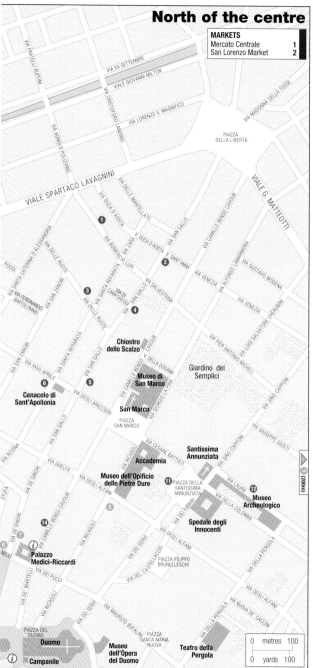

MARKETS	
Mercato Centrale	1
San Lorenzo Market	2

VIA FRATELLI RUFFINI

VIA XX SETTEMBRE

VIALE GIOVANNI MILTON

VIA CRISTOFORO LANDINO

VIA LORENZO IL MAGNIFICO

VIA MADONNA DELLA TOSSE

PIAZZA DELLA LIBERTÀ

VIA AGNOLO POLIZIANO

VIALE SPARTACO LAVAGNINI

VIA DUCA D'AOSTA

VIA DELLE MANTELLATE

VIALE G. MATTEOTTI

POGGI

VIA SANTA CATERINA D'ALESSANDRIA

VIA DELLE RUOTE

VIA BONFACIO LUPI

VIA ZARA

VIA DUCA D'AOSTA

VIA SAN GALLO

V. SANT'ANNA

VIA CAMILLO BENSO CAVOUR

VIA ALFONSO LAMARMORA

VIA GUSTAVO MODENA

VIA FERNANDO BARTOLOMMEI

VIA SAN ZANOBI

VIA SANTA REPARATA

VIA DI CAMPOREGGI

VIA SAN GALLO

VIA SALVESTRINA

VIA SANT'ANNA

VIA VENEZIA

VIA DELLE RUOTE

VIA VENEZIA

VIA PIER ANTONIO MICHELI

VIA LUIGI SALVATORE CHERUBINI

Chiostro dello Scalzo

VIA SAN GALLO

VIA SAN ZANOBI

VIA XXVII APRILE

VIA SANTA REPARATA

VIA SAN GALLO

VIA CAMILLO BENSO CAVOUR

V. DELLA DOGANA

Giardino dei Semplici

Cenacolo di Sant'Apollonia

Museo di San Marco

VIA DEGLI ARAZZIERI

VIA GIORGIO LA PIRA

VIA GINO CAPPONI

San Marco

PIAZZA SAN MARCO

VIA GIUSEPPE GIUSTI

VIA RICASOLI

VIA CESARE BATTISTI

Santissima Annunziata

(200m)

VIA RICASOLI

Accademia

VIA GINO CAPPONI

VIA RISINA

VIA GUELFA

Museo dell'Opificio delle Pietre Dure

VIA DEGLI ALFANI

PIAZZA DELLA SANTISSIMA ANNUNZIATA

VIA LAURA

Museo Archeologico

VIA DELLA COLONNA

STUFA

VIA DE GINORI

VIA DE' SERVI

VIA DELLA PERGOLA

VIA CAMILLO BENSO CAVOUR

VIA RICASOLI

Spedale degli Innocenti

VIA DEGLI ALFANI

VIA DE GINORI

Palazzo Medici-Riccardi

VIA DEI PUCCI

VIA DE' SERVI

VIA DEL CASTELLACCIO

PIAZZA FILIPPO BRUNELLESCHI

VIA DEGLI ALFANI

VIA NUOVA DE' CACCINI

VIA DE' MARTELLI

VIA RICASOLI

VIA MAURIZIO BUFALINI

PIAZZA SANTA MARIA NUOVA

VIA DELLA PERGOLA

PIAZZA DEL DUOMO

Duomo

Museo dell'Opera del Duomo

Teatro della Pergola

Campanile

0	metres	100
0	yards	100

Sagrestia Nuova, Cappelle Medicee

colourful stone-plated hall built as a mausoleum for Cosimo I and the grand dukes who succeeded him. Pass straight through for the **Sagrestia Nuova**, which was designed by Michelangelo as a tribute to Brunelleschi's Sagrestia Vecchia in the main body of San Lorenzo. The architecture plays complex games with the visual vocabulary of classical architecture, and provides a magnificent setting for the three **Medici tombs** (1520–34), two of which are wholly by Michelangelo and the other one partly.

The tomb on the left as you enter belongs to Lorenzo, Duke of Urbino, grandson of Lorenzo the Magnificent. Michelangelo depicts him as a man of thought, and his sarcophagus bears figures of *Dawn* and *Dusk*, the times of day whose ambiguities appeal to the contemplative mind. Opposite stands the tomb of Lorenzo de' Medici's youngest son, Giuliano, Duke of Nemours; as a man of action, his character is symbolized by the clear antithesis of *Day* and *Night*.

The two principal effigies were intended to face the equally grand tombs of Lorenzo de' Medici and his brother Giuliano. The only part of the project completed by Michelangelo is the *Madonna and Child*, the last image of the Madonna he ever sculpted. The figures to either side are Cosmas and Damian, patron saints of doctors (*medici*) and the Medici. Although completed by others, they follow Michelangelo's design.

Casa Martelli

MAP PAGE 68, POCKET MAP D4
Via Zannetti 8.
Ⓦ bargellomusei.beniculturali.it. Free.
From the sixteenth century until the death of the last of the Martelli in 1989, **Casa Martelli** was home to a family that for many years was very closely associated with their near neighbours, the Medici. It was not until 1738 that Casa Martelli took on its present form, when several houses were merged to create this spectacular palazzo. The interior was then completely redecorated, and it's the style of this refurbishment

that dominates, with room after room of trompe l'oeil frescoes, sumptuous furniture, delicate stucco work and shimmering brocades. The family's art collection, stacked almost to the ceiling in the picture gallery, includes work by Piero di Cosimo, Salvator Rosa and Luca Giordano.

The Palazzo Medici-Riccardi

MAP PAGE 68, POCKET MAP E4
Via Cavour 1. Ⓦ palazzomediciriccardi.it. Charge.

The **Palazzo Medici-Riccardi** was built for Cosimo de' Medici by Michelozzo between 1444 and 1462, and remained the family headquarters until Cosimo I moved to the Palazzo Vecchio (see page 38) in 1540. In Cosimo de Medici's prime, around fifty members of the clan lived here; Donatello's *Judith and Holofernes* (now in the Palazzo Vecchio) adorned the walled garden, while the same artist's *David* (now in the Bargello) stood in the entrance courtyard.

The palace now houses the offices of the provincial government, but you can visit parts of it, notably the chapel and its **cycle of frescoes**, which a maximum of fifteen may view at one time.

Painted around 1460, Benozzo Gozzoli's frescoes of *The Journey of the Magi* probably portray the pageant of the Compagnia dei Magi, the most patrician of the city's religious confraternities, whose annual procession took place at Epiphany. Several Medici were prominent members, including Piero de' Medici (Piero il Gottoso), who may have commissioned the pictures. It's known that several of the Medici household are featured in the procession, but putting names to these prettified faces is a problem. The man leading the cavalcade on a white horse is almost certainly Piero. Lorenzo il Magnifico, 11 years old at the time

the fresco was painted, is probably the young king in the foreground, riding the grey horse detached from the rest of the procession, while his brother, Giuliano, is most likely the one preceded by the black bowman. The artist himself is in the crowd on the far left, his red beret signed with the words "Opus Benotii" in gold.

Another set of stairs leads up to the **first floor**, where a display case in the lobby of the main gallery contains a *Madonna and Child* (late 1460s) by Filippo Lippi. The ceiling of the grandiloquent **gallery** glows with Luca Giordano's fresco of *The Apotheosis of the Medici* (1683), from which one can only deduce that Giordano had no sense of shame. Accompanying Cosimo III on his flight into the ether is his son, the last male Medici, Gian Gastone, who grew to be a man so inert that he could rarely summon the energy to get out of bed in the morning.

The Mercato Centrale

MAP PAGE 68, POCKET MAP D3
Piazza del Mercato Centrale.
Ⓦ mercatocentrale.com/florence.

The **Mercato Centrale** was designed by Giuseppe Mengoni, architect of Milan's famous Galleria, and is one of Europe's largest covered food halls. Butchers, *alimentari*, tripe-sellers, greengrocers – they're all gathered under the one roof, along with some excellent *tavole calde* – serving sandwiches and basic lunches – of which *Da Nerbone* is the most famous. Opened in 1874, the Mercato Centrale received an overhaul a century later, reopening in 1980 with a new first floor; in 2014 another restoration transformed the upper level into a sort of indoor piazza with bars and eateries.

The San Lorenzo street market, which used to spread into Piazza San Lorenzo, is now confined to the streets immediately

Michelangelo

Michelangelo Buonarroti (1475–1564) was born in Caprese in eastern Tuscany, but his family soon moved to Florence, where he became a pupil of Ghirlandaio, making his first stone reliefs for Lorenzo de' Medici. After the Medici were expelled from the city the young Michelangelo went to Rome in 1496. There he secured a reputation as the **most skilled sculptor** of his day with the *Bacchus* (now in the Bargello) and the *Pietà* for St Peter's.

After his return to Florence in 1501, Michelangelo carved the *David* and the *St Matthew* (both in the Accademia). He was also employed to paint a fresco of the *Battle of Cascina* in the Palazzo Vecchio. Only the cartoon was finished, but this became the single most influential work of art in the city, its twisting nudes a recurrent motif in later Mannerist art. Work was suspended in 1505 when Michelangelo was called to Rome by Pope Julius II to create his tomb; the *Slaves* in the Accademia was intended for this grandiose project which, like many of Michelangelo's schemes, was never finished.

In 1508 Michelangelo began his other superhuman project, the decoration of the **Sistine Chapel** ceiling in Rome. Back in Florence, he started work on the San Lorenzo complex in 1516, staying on to supervise its defences when it was besieged by the Medici and Charles V in 1530. Four years later he left Florence for good, and spent his last thirty years in Rome, during which he produced the *Last Judgement* in the Sistine Chapel. Florence has one work from this final phase of Michelangelo's career, the *Pietà* he intended for his own tomb (now in the Museo dell'Opera del Duomo; see page 31).

surrounding the Mercato Centrale. Every day from 8am to 7pm this area is thronged with stalls selling bags, belts, leather jackets and football shirts. Quality isn't the highest, but prices are fairly low.

The Fortezza da Basso

MAP PAGE 68, POCKET MAP C1–C2
Piazza Adua.

The **Fortezza da Basso** was built to intimidate the people of Florence by the vile Alessandro de' Medici, who ordained himself duke of Florence after a ten-month siege by the army of Charles V and Pope Clement VII (possibly Alessandro's father) had forcibly restored the Medici. Within a few years the cruelties of Alessandro had become intolerable; a petition to Charles V spoke of the Fortezza da Basso as "a prison and a slaughterhouse

for the unhappy citizens". Charles's response to Alessandro's atrocities was to marry his daughter to the tyrant. In the end, another Medici came to the rescue: in 1537 the distantly related Lorenzaccio de' Medici stabbed the duke to death. Subsequently the Fortezza da Basso fell into dereliction, but since 1978 it has been used for trade fairs and shows such as the Pitti Moda fashion jamborees in January and July; the city's main art-restoration workshops are here too.

The Cenacolo di Sant'Apollonia

MAP PAGE 68, POCKET MAP E3
Via XXVII Aprile 1. Free.

Most of the former Benedictine convent of Sant'Apollonia has now been turned into apartments, but the lower part of an entire wall of the former refectory is taken up with Andrea del Castagno's disturbing *Last Supper* (c.1447). Blood-red is the dominant tone, and the most commanding figure is the diabolic, black-bearded Judas, who sits on the near side of the table. The seething patterns in the marbled panels behind the Apostles seem to mimic the turmoil in the mind of each as he hears Christ's announcement of the betrayal. Castagno also painted the *Crucifixion*, *Deposition* and *Resurrection* above the illusionistic space in which the Last Supper takes place, and the *Crucifixion* and *Pietà* on the adjacent walls.

The Accademia

MAP PAGE 68, POCKET MAP F3
Via Ricasoli 66.
Ⓦ galleriaaccademiafirenze.it. Charge.
The **Galleria dell'Accademia** has an extensive collection of paintings, but what draws the crowds is the sculpture of **Michelangelo**, in particular the *David*. So great is the public appetite for this one work in particular that you'd be advised

to book tickets in advance (see page 133).

Commissioned by the Opera del Duomo in 1501, the *David* was conceived to invoke parallels with Florence's recent liberation from Savonarola and the Medici. It's an incomparable show of technical bravura, all the more impressive given the difficulties posed by the marble from which it was carved. The four-metre block of stone – thin, shallow and riddled with cracks – had been quarried from Carrara forty years earlier. Several artists had already attempted to work with it, notably Leonardo da Vinci. Michelangelo succeeded where others had failed, completing the work in 1504 when he was still just 29. Displayed for almost four hundred years in the Piazza della Signoria, the *David* today occupies a specially built alcove, protected by a glass barrier that was built in 1991, after one of its toes was vandalized with a hammer. In 2004 he was given a thorough cleaning for the first time in decades, restoring the gangly youth to something like his original brilliance.

Michelangelo's *David*

Fra' Angelico fresco, San Marco

Michelangelo once described the process of carving as being the liberation of the form from within the stone, a notion that seems to be embodied by the unfinished **Slaves** (or Prisoners). His procedure, clearly demonstrated here, was to cut the figure as if it were a deep relief, and then to free the three-dimensional figure; often his assistants would perform the initial operation, so it's possible that Michelangelo's own chisel never actually touched these stones. Probably carved in the late 1520s, the statues were originally destined for the tomb of Julius II, a project that was eventually abandoned; four of the original six statues came to the Accademia in 1909, while two others found their way to the Louvre.

Close by is another unfinished work, *St Matthew* (1505–06), started soon after completion of the *David* as a commission from the Opera del Duomo; they actually requested a full series of the Apostles from Michelangelo, but this is the only one he ever began.

The **picture galleries** that flank the main sculpture hall are generally unexciting, with copious examples of the work of "Unknown Florentine" and "Follower of …". The pieces likeliest to make an impact are Pontormo's *Venus and Cupid* (1532), painted to a cartoon by Michelangelo; a *Madonna of the Sea* (1470) attributed to Botticelli; and the painted fifteenth-century *Adimari Chest*, showing a Florentine wedding ceremony in the Piazza del Duomo.

The Museo dell'Opificio delle Pietre Dure

MAP PAGE 68, POCKET MAP F3
Via degli Alfani 78.
Ⓦ opificiodellepietredure.cultura.gov.it.
Charge.

Occupying a corner of the Accademia building, the **Opificio delle Pietre Dure** was founded in 1588 to train craftsmen in the distinctively Florentine art of creating pictures or patterns with highly polished, inlaid **semi-precious stones**. The museum clearly elucidates the highly skilled processes involved in the creation of *pietre dure* work, and has some remarkable examples of the genre. If you want to see some more spectacular (and rather gross) specimens, you should visit the Cappelle Medicee (see page 67). While local workshops still maintain the traditions of this specialized art-form, the Opificio itself has evolved into one of the world's leading centres for the restoration of artworks.

The Museo di San Marco

MAP PAGE 68, POCKET MAP F3
Piazza San Marco. Charge.

Much of the north side of Piazza San Marco is taken up by the Dominican convent of San Marco, now the home of the **Museo di San Marco**. The Dominicans acquired the site in 1436, and the complex promptly became the recipient of Cosimo de' Medici's most lavish patronage. Ironically, the convent became the centre of resistance to the Medici later in the century: Girolamo Savonarola, leader of the government of Florence after the expulsion of the Medici in 1494, was the prior of San Marco.

During the Medici-funded rebuilding, the convent was decorated by one of its friars and a future prior, Fra' Angelico, a Tuscan painter in whom a medieval simplicity of faith was uniquely allied to a Renaissance sophistication of manner. Twenty or so paintings by the artist are gathered in the ground-floor **Ospizio dei Pellegrini**, or Pilgrims' Hospice, including several of Angelico's most famous creations. Here you'll see a wonderful *Deposition* that originally hung in the church of Santa Trìnita, the *Madonna dei Linaiuoli* (1433), which was Angelico's first major public painting, and the so-called *Pala di San Marco* (1440), a painting that has been badly damaged by the passage of time and a disastrous restoration, but demonstrates Fra' Angelico's familiarity with the principle of a central vanishing point, as expounded in Alberti's *Della Pittura*

(*On Painting*), published in Italian just two years before the picture was executed.

Elsewhere on ground level you'll find Fra' Bartolomeo's portrait of Savonarola, his unfinished *Pala della Signoria*, and – in the **Sala Capitolare**, or Chapter House – a powerful fresco of the *Crucifixion*, painted by Angelico and assistants. Most of the main cloister's frescoes are sixteenth-century depictions of episodes from the life of Antonino Pierozzi, Fra' Angelico's mentor, who was canonized as St Antonine in 1523; Fra' Angelico himself painted the frescoes in its four corners. Before going upstairs, make sure you also see the **Refettorio Piccolo**, or Small Refectory, which has a lustrous *Last Supper* (1480) by Ghirlandaio.

At the top of the stairs you're confronted with one of the most sublime paintings in Italy: for the drama of its setting and the lucidity of its composition, nothing in San Marco matches Angelico's *Annunciation*. Angelico and his assistants also painted the simple and piously restrained pictures in each of the 44 **dormitory cells** on this floor, into which the friars would withdraw for solitary contemplation and sleep. Several of the scenes include one or both of a pair of monastic onlookers, serving as intermediaries between the occupant of the cell and the personages in the pictures: the one with the star above his head is St Dominic; the one with the split skull is St Peter Martyr.

The rooms once occupied by Savonarola now contain various relics questionably authenticated as worn by the man himself; the more luxuriously appointed cells 29 and 30 were the personal domain of Cosimo de' Medici – the fresco of the *Adoration of the Magi* may have been suggested by Cosimo himself, who liked to think of himself as a latter-day wise man and gift-giving king.

Main cloister, San Marco

On the way to these VIP cells you'll pass the entrance to **Michelozzo's Library**, built in 1441–44 to a design that exudes an atmosphere of calm study. Cosimo's agents roamed as far as the Near East garnering precious manuscripts and books for him; in turn, Cosimo handed all the religious items over to the monastery, stipulating that they should be accessible to all, making this Europe's first **public library**. As the plaque by the doorway tells you, it was on this spot that Savonarola was arrested in 1498.

San Marco church

MAP PAGE 68, POCKET MAP F3
Piazza San Marco. Free.

The **church** of San Marco is worth a quick visit for two works on the second and third altars on the right: a *Madonna and Saints* painted in 1509 by Fra' Bartolomeo, and an eighth-century mosaic of *The Madonna in Prayer* (surrounded by later additions), brought here from Rome. This had to be cut in half in transit, and you can still see the break across the Virgin's midriff. The preserved body

of St Antonine lies in a chapel designed by Giambologna, and the great Renaissance humanists Pico della Mirandola and Poliziano are entombed in the left wall of the nave, above the statue of Savonarola.

The Chiostro dello Scalzo

MAP PAGE 68, POCKET MAP F2
Via Cavour 69. Free.

Lo Scalzo was the home of the **Brotherhood of St John**, whose vows of poverty entailed walking around barefoot (*scalzo*). The order was suppressed in 1785 and their monastery sold off, except for the cloister, which was the training ground for Andrea del Sarto; his monochrome paintings of *The Cardinal Virtues* and *Scenes from the Life of the Baptist* occupied him off and on for a decade from 1511. A couple of the sixteen scenes – *John in the Wilderness* and *John meeting Christ* – were executed by his pupil Franciabigio in 1518, when del Sarto was away in Paris.

The Giardino dei Semplici

MAP PAGE 68, POCKET MAP F3
Via La Pira. Charge.

The **Giardino dei Semplici** or Orto Botanico – the nearest equivalent to the Bóboli garden on the north side of the city – was set up in 1545 for Cosimo I as a **medicinal garden**, following the examples of Padua and Pisa, and now covers five acres, most of the area being taken up by the original flowerbeds and avenues. The **university museums** that adjoin the Giardino dei Semplici – the Museo Botanico, the Museo di Minerologia e Litologia and the Museo di Geologia e Paleontologia – are of specialist interest.

Piazza Santissima Annunziata

MAP PAGE 68, POCKET MAP F3–F4

Nineteenth-century urban renewal schemes left many of Florence's squares rather grim places, which makes the pedestrianized **Piazza Santissima Annunziata**, with its distinctive **arcades**, all the more attractive a public space. It has a special importance for the city, too. Until the end of the eighteenth century the Florentine year used to begin on March 25, the Festival of the Annunciation – hence the Florentine predilection for paintings of the Annunciation, and the fashionableness of the Annunziata church, which has long been the place for big weddings. The festival is still marked by a huge fair in the piazza and the streets leading off it; later in the year, on the first weekend in September, the square is used for Tuscany's largest crafts fair.

   Brunelleschi began the piazza in the 1420s, with additions made later by Ammannati and Antonio da Sangallo. The equestrian statue of Grand Duke Ferdinando I (1608) at its centre was Giambologna's final work, and was cast by his pupil Pietro Tacca, from cannons captured at the Battle of Lepanto. Tacca was also the creator of the two bizarre **fountains**, on each of which a pair of aquatic monkeys spit water at two whiskered sea slugs.

The Spedale degli Innocenti

MAP PAGE 68, POCKET MAP F4
Piazza Santissima Annunziata. Charge.

Piazza Santissima Annunziata's most elegant building is the **Spedale degli Innocenti**, or Ospedale. Commissioned in 1419 by the Arte della Seta, the silk-weavers' guild, it opened in 1445 as the first foundlings' hospital in Europe, and is still an **orphanage** today. It was largely designed by Brunelleschi, and his nine-arched loggia was one of Europe's earliest examples of the new classically influenced style. (The building on the other side of the piazza was designed a century later, by Antonio da Sangallo and Baccio d'Agnolo, as accommodation for the Servite friars who staffed the orphanage.) Andrea della Robbia's blue-backed ceramic tondi of well-swaddled babies advertise the building's function, but their gaiety belies the misery associated with it. Slavery was part of the

Giambologna's statue of Grand Duke Ferdinando I in Piazza Santissima Annunziata

The Chimera in the Museo Archeologico

Florentine economy as late as the fifteenth century (it's probable that Leonardo da Vinci's mother was a slave), and many of the infants given to the care of the Spedale were born to domestic slaves. From 1660 children could be abandoned anonymously in the *rota*, a small revolving door whose bricked-up remains are still visible at the extreme left of the facade; it remained in use until 1875.

The Museo degli Innocenti reopened in 2016 after a major renovation, and now comprises three sections. New exhibition space in the basement is devoted to the history and work of the Instituto degli Innocenti. On the ground floor, the focus is on two beautiful cloisters, Brunelleschi's Cortile degli Uomini (Men's Court) and the graceful Cortile delle Donne (Women's Court). Upstairs, the gallery contains a miscellany of Florentine Renaissance art that includes one of Luca della Robbia's most beguiling Madonnas and an *Adoration of the Magi* (1488) by Domenico Ghirlandaio. The smartened-up Spedale now has

a café on the top floor, with a panoramic terrace.

Santissima Annunziata

MAP PAGE 68, POCKET MAP F3
Piazza Santissima Annunziata. Free.
Santissima Annunziata is the mother church of the **Servites**, or Servi di Maria (Servants of Mary), a religious order founded by Filippo Benizzi and six Florentine aristocrats in 1234. From humble beginnings, the order blossomed after 1252, when a painting of the Virgin begun by one of the monks but abandoned in despair because of his inability to create a truly beautiful image, was supposedly completed by an angel while he slept. So many people came to venerate the image that by 1444 a new church, financed by the Medici, was commissioned from Michelozzo, who happened to be the brother of the Servites' head prior.

As the number of pilgrims to the church increased, so it became a custom to leave wax votive offerings (*voti*) in honour of its miraculous Madonna. These became so numerous that in 1447 a special atrium, the **Chiostrino** dei Voti, was built onto the church, and in 1516 a major fresco cycle was commissioned, on the occasion of the canonization of Filippo Benizzi. Three leading artists of the day, Andrea del Sarto, Jacopo Pontormo and Rosso Fiorentino, were involved, together with several lesser painters. Some of the panels are in a poor state – all were removed from the walls and restored after the 1966 flood (see page 83) – but their overall effect is superb.

Just inside the church itself, on the left, stands the ornate tabernacle (1448–61) designed by Michelozzo to house the miraculous image of the Madonna. The nearby **Cappella Feroni** features a fresco by Andrea del Castagno of *Christ and St Julian* (1455–56); a more striking fresco by the same artist, *The Holy Trinity and St Jerome* (1454), can be seen in the adjacent chapel. Now restored, both frescoes were obliterated after Vasari spread the rumour that Castagno had poisoned his erstwhile friend, Domenico Veneziano, motivated by envy of the other's skill with oil paint. Castagno was saddled with this crime until the nineteenth century, when an archivist discovered that the alleged murderer in fact predeceased his victim by four years. The church's other notable painting is Andrea del Sarto's intimate *Madonna del Sacco* (1525) in the spacious **Chiostro dei Morti**, over the door that opens from the north transept (you may need to find the sacristan to open it); the picture – more formally known as *Rest during the Flight into Egypt* – takes its curious name from the sack on which St Joseph is leaning.

The Museo Archeologico

MAP PAGE 68, POCKET MAP F3–G4
Via della Colonna 36. Charge.

The special strength of the **Museo Archeologico** is its Etruscan collection, much of it bequeathed, inevitably, by the Medici. Most of the finds are on the first floor, where there's a large array of funerary figures and two outstanding bronze sculptures: the *Arringatore* (Orator), the only known large Etruscan bronze from the Hellenistic period, made some time around 100 BC; and the *Chimera*, a triple-headed monster made in the fourth century BC.

Numerous dowdy cabinets are stuffed with unlabelled Etruscan figurines, and much of the **Egyptian collection** is displayed in a similarly uninspiring manner. The single most remarkable object amid the assembly of papyri, statuettes and mummy cases is a Hittite chariot made of bone and wood, dating from the fourteenth century BC.

There are more Etruscan pieces on the top floor (sometimes open only to guided tours), but here the primary focus is on the **Greek and Roman collections**. The star piece in the huge hoard of Greek vases is the large *François Vase*, a sixth-century BC *krater*. Another attention-grabbing item is the life-size bronze torso known as the *Torso di Livorno*, either a fifth-century BC Greek original or a Roman copy. There's some debate also about the large horse's head that's on show in the same room. This fragment of a full-size statue is probably an early Hellenistic bronze from around 100 BC, but again it may be a Roman copy; what's known for certain is that it was once in the garden of the Palazzo Medici, where it was studied by Donatello and Verrocchio. Also on this floor you'll see two beautiful sixth-century BC Greek *kouroi*, dubbed *Apollo* and *Apollino*, and the bronze statue of a young man known as the *Idolino di Pésaro* – it's generally thought to be a Roman replica of a Greek figure dating from around 100 BC.

Markets

Mercato Centrale

MAP PAGE 68, POCKET MAP D3
Piazza del Mercato Centrale.

The vast food hall is great for
picnic supplies, but also well
worth a sightseeing and people-
watching visit whether you
intend to buy anything or not.
Da Nerbone, one of the market's
excellent *tavole calde*, serves
meatballs, pasta, stews, soups,
salads and sandwiches – perfect
for a simple but hearty lunch. The
upper floor of the market has a
pizzeria, a *birreria*, a wine bar and
various other places to eat and
drink, which keep the building
lively long after the market stalls
have shut down for the day.

San Lorenzo Market

MAP PAGE 68, POCKET MAP D4
Piazza di San Lorenzo.

A vast open-air warehouse of cheap
clothing, bags and belts. If you're
looking for a low-price replica

Fiorentina shirt or a bargain leather
jacket, this is the place.

Cafés & bars

Casa del Vino

MAP PAGE 68, POCKET MAP D4
Via dell'Ariento 16r.
Ⓦ facebook.com/migliorinigianni.

Located a few yards from the
Mercato Centrale, this wine bar
is thronged at lunchtime with
traders who pitch up for a drink,
a chat with friendly owner Gianni
Migliorini and a few panini or
crostini. €

Enoteca de'Giusti

MAP PAGE 68, POCKET MAP G4
Via Giuseppe Giusti 2r.
Ⓦ enotecadegiusti.com.

Run by the same people who own
Pitti Gola e Cantina on the other
side of town (see page 106), this
friendly little place has a lovely
atmosphere, tasty dishes and a
wide choice of excellent wines to
boot. €

Handbags for sale, San Lorenzo Market

La Ménagère

MAP PAGE 68, POCKET MAP E4
Via de' Ginori 8r. Ⓦ lamenagere.it.
Formerly a market hall, this building has been spectacularly refashioned as a bar-bistro-restaurant-café, with a home accessories boutique and a florist on the premises too. Rusty tables and unplastered walls set a tone of distressed chic, and the vaulted dining room, with its single 18-metre table, is amazing. *La Ménagère* is perhaps best, however, as a place for a morning coffee, a light lunch or a late-night drink. €

Zanobini

MAP PAGE 68, POCKET MAP D4
Via Sant'Antonino 47r. ☎ 055 239 6850.
Like the nearby *Casa del Vino* this is an authentic and long-established place, but here the emphasis is more on the wine: few bars in Florence have a better selection. €

Gelateria

Carabé

MAP PAGE 68, POCKET MAP E4
Via Ricasoli 60r. ☎ 055 289 476.
Wonderful Sicilian ice cream made with Sicilian ingredients as only they know how. Try the *Spirito Siciliano* flavour – the most lemony lemon you'll ever taste. Also serves delicious *cannoli* (pastry stuffed with sweet ricotta and candied fruits). €

Restaurants

Da Mario

MAP PAGE 68, POCKET MAP E3
Via Rosina 2r. Ⓦ trattoriamario.com.
For earthy Florentine cooking at low prices, there's nowhere better than *Da Mario*, which has been in operation since 1953. In the past it closed at 3pm which seemed a great shame to its customers; to the delight of its patrons in 2020

Zà-Zà, a local institution

it decided to put on an extra shift on Thursday and Friday evenings. €

Sergio Gozzi

MAP PAGE 68, POCKET MAP E4
Piazza San Lorenzo 8r. ☎ 055 281 941.
This plain bar-trattoria, lurking behind the San Lorenzo market stalls, is a good choice for an inexpensive lunch, with a short and simple menu that changes daily. It doesn't take reservations. €

Zà-Zà

MAP PAGE 68, POCKET MAP E3
Piazza del Mercato Centrale 26r. Ⓦ trattoriazaza.it.
In business for more than forty years, *Zà-Zà* has become a guidebook mainstay, and though it's now a much bigger operation than it used to be (it occupies most of one side of the piazza), it's still one of the best trattorias close to the Mercato Centrale. The menu has lots of salads, seafood dishes and Tuscan meats. €

East of the centre

The vast Franciscan church of Santa Croce is one of the most compelling sights in Florence, and forms the centrepiece of an area which, prior to the terrible flood of 1966, was one of the city's more densely populated districts. When the Arno burst its banks, this low-lying quarter, packed with tenements and small workshops, was virtually wrecked, and many of its residents moved out permanently in the following years. Now, however, the district has revived in a big way, and it's here that you'll find many of the city's liveliest bars and best restaurants. In addition to the mighty Santa Croce, the district's cultural attractions are the Museo Horne, the Casa Buonarroti, and a brace of smaller churches.

Santa Croce

MAP PAGE 84, POCKET MAP F6–G6
Piazza Santa Croce. Ⓦ santacroceopera.it.
Charge, extra for tour.

The church of **Santa Croce** is the Franciscans' principal church in Florence and is said to have been founded by St Francis himself. In truth it was probably begun seventy or so years after Francis's death, in 1294, possibly by the architect of the Duomo, Arnolfo di Cambio. Ironically, it was the city's richest families who funded the construction of the church: plutocrats such as the Bardi, Peruzzi and Baroncelli sponsored the extraordinary **fresco cycles** that were lavished on the chapels over the years, particularly during the fourteenth century, when artists of the stature of Giotto and the Gaddi family worked here. And Santa Croce has long served as the national pantheon: it contains monuments to more than 270 illustrious Italians, including Michelangelo, Galileo, Machiavelli and Dante (though the last is not buried here).

On your way to the frescoed chapels be sure to take a look at Donatello's gilded stone relief of the *Annunciation* (against the right-hand wall) and Bernardo Rossellino's nearby tomb of Leonardo Bruni, chancellor of the Republic, humanist scholar and author of the first history of the city. (His successor as chancellor, Carlo Marsuppini, is commemorated by a splendid tomb in the opposite aisle, carved by Desiderio da Settignano.) The **Cappella Castellani**, at the end of the south aisle, was strikingly frescoed by Agnolo Gaddi and his pupils, while the adjoining **Cappella Baroncelli** was decorated by Agnolo's father, Taddeo, a long-time assistant to Giotto.

Both the **Cappella Peruzzi** and the **Cappella Bardi** – the two chapels on the right of the chancel – are covered with frescoes by Giotto, with some assistance in the latter. Their deterioration was partly caused by Giotto's having painted some of the pictures onto dry plaster, but the vandalism of later generations was far more destructive. Scenes from the lives of St John the Evangelist and St John the Baptist fill the Peruzzi chapel, while a better-preserved cycle of the life of St Francis fills the Bardi. Despite the areas of paint destroyed when a tomb was attached to the wall, the *Funeral of St Francis* is still a composition of extraordinary impact, the grief-stricken mourners suggesting an affinity with the lamentation over the body of Christ – one of them even probes the wound in Francis's side, echoing the gesture of Doubting Thomas.

Florence's floods

Calamitous floods are nothing new in Florence. Great areas of the city were destroyed by floodwater in 1178, and in 1269 the Carraia and Trìnita bridges were carried away on a torrent so heavy that "a great part of the city of Florence became a lake", as a contemporary chronicler put it. Bridges were also destroyed by the raging Arno in 1333, and Cosimo I instituted an urban beautification scheme after a flood put nearly twenty feet of muddy water over parts of the city in 1557; on that occasion the Trìnita bridge was hit so suddenly that everyone on it was drowned, except for a couple of children who were left stranded on a pillar in midstream, where for two days they were fed by means of a rope slung over from the bank.

It rained continuously for forty days prior to November 4, **1966**, with nearly half a metre of rain falling in the preceding two days. When the water pressure in an upstream reservoir threatened to break the dam, it was decided to open the sluices. The only people to be warned about the rapidly rising level of the river were the jewellers of the Ponte Vecchio, whose private nightwatchman phoned them in the small hours of the morning with news that the bridge was starting to shake. When the banks of the Arno finally broke, a flash flood dumped around 500,000 tonnes of water and mud on the streets, moving with such speed that people were drowned in the underpass of Santa Maria Novella train station. In all, 35 Florentines were killed, 6000 shops put out of business, more than 10,000 homes made uninhabitable, some 15,000 cars wrecked, and thousands of works of art damaged, many of them ruined by heating oil flushed out of basements.

Within hours an impromptu army of rescue workers had been formed to haul pictures out of slime-filled churches and gather fragments of paint in plastic bags. Donations came in from all over the world, but the task was so immense that the restoration of many items is still continuing – scores of precious books from the National Library, which is located next door to Santa Croce and took the brunt of the flood, remain in the laboratories. In total around two-thirds of the 3000 paintings damaged in the flood are now on view again (including the great **Cimabue Crucifix**, which has become an emblem of the disaster), and two laboratories – one for paintings and one for stonework – are operating full time in Florence, developing restoration techniques that are taken up by galleries all over the world. Today, throughout the city, you can see small marble plaques with a red line showing the level the floodwaters reached on that dreadful day in 1966. The flood is rendered exquisitely in Sarah Winman's historical novel *Still Life*, which is a big-hearted book set in the city; a true love letter to twentieth-century Florence.

From the right transept a corridor leads to the **Cappella Medici**, which contains Bronzino's huge *Descent of Christ into Limbo* and an altarpiece by Andrea and Giovanni della Robbia. Adjoining the corridor, the beautifully panelled sacristy is home to Cimabue's great *Crucifix*, which was half-destroyed in the 1966 flood and has become in effect the emblem of that disaster.

On the other side of the church there's a second **Cappella Bardi**, which houses a wooden crucifix by Donatello, supposedly criticized by Brunelleschi as resembling a "peasant on the Cross".

The door in the right aisle leads through into the church's Primo Chiostro (First Cloister), site of Brunelleschi's **Cappella Pazzi**, the epitome of the learned, harmonious spirit of early Renaissance architecture, with lovely terracotta work by Luca della Robbia and his workshop.

The **Museo dell'Opera di Santa Croce**, flanking the first cloister, houses a miscellany of works, including Donatello's gilded *St Louis of Toulouse* (1424). Next door is the serene **Inner Cloister,** another late project by Brunelleschi.

Casa Buonarroti

MAP PAGE 84, POCKET MAP G6
Via Ghibellina 70. ⓦ casabuonarroti.it.
Charge.

The enticing name of the **Casa Buonarroti** is somewhat misleading: **Michelangelo Buonarroti** certainly owned three houses here in 1508, and probably lived on the site intermittently between 1516 and 1525, but on Michelangelo's death they passed to his nephew, whose son converted them into a single palazzo, leaving little trace of the earlier houses. Michelangelo's last descendant, Cosimo, left the building to the city on his death in 1858. Today

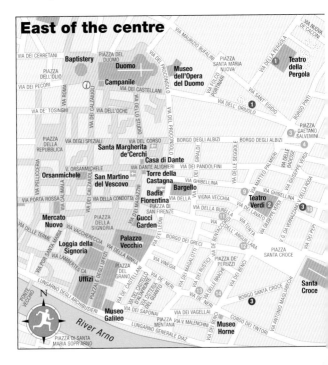

the house contains a smart but low-key **museum**, nicely decorated in period style and adorned with beautiful furniture, objets d'art, frescoed ceilings and the like, but only a handful of the works of art on display are by Michelangelo. The *Madonna della Scala* (c.1490–92) is Michelangelo's earliest known work, a delicate relief carved when he was no older than 16. The similarly unfinished *Battle of the Centaurs* was created shortly afterwards, when he was living in the Medici household. In the adjacent room you'll find the artist's wooden model (1517) for the facade of San Lorenzo, close to the largest of all the sculptural models on display, the torso of a *River God* (1524), a work probably intended for the Medici chapel in San Lorenzo. Other rooms contain small and fragmentary pieces, possibly by the master, possibly copies of works by him.

Sant'Ambrogio

MAP PAGE 84, POCKET MAP H5
Piazza di Sant'Ambrogio. Free.

Sant'Ambrogio is one of Florence's oldest churches, having been documented in 988, though rebuilding over the centuries has resulted in a somewhat bland appearance. Inside you'll find a *Madonna Enthroned with SS John the Baptist and Bartholomew* (second altar on the right), attributed to Orcagna (or the school of Orcagna), and a recently restored triptych in the chapel to the right of the main altar, attributed to Lorenzo di Bicci or Bicci di Lorenzo. More compelling than either painting, though, is the **Cappella del Miracolo**, the chapel to the left of the high altar, and its tabernacle (1481–83) by Mino da Fiesole, an accomplished sculptor whose name crops up time and again across Tuscany. This was one of Mino's last works – he died in 1484 – making

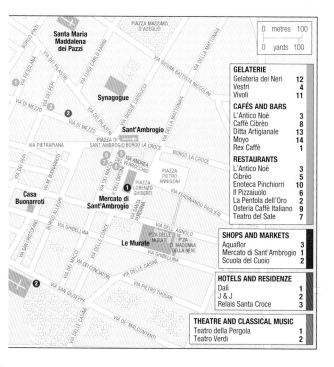

GELATERIE	
Gelateria dei Neri	12
Vestri	4
Vivoli	11

CAFÉS AND BARS	
L'Antico Noè	3
Caffè Cibrèo	8
Ditta Artigianale	13
Moyo	14
Rex Caffè	1

RESTAURANTS	
L'Antico Noè	3
Cibrèo	5
Enoteca Pinchiorri	10
Il Pizzaiuolo	6
La Pentola dell'Oro	2
Osteria Caffè Italiano	9
Teatro del Sale	7

SHOPS AND MARKETS	
Aquaflor	3
Mercato di Sant'Ambrogio	1
Scuola del Cuoio	2

HOTELS AND RESIDENZE	
Dalì	1
J & J	2
Relais Santa Croce	3

THEATRE AND CLASSICAL MUSIC	
Teatro della Pergola	1
Teatro Verdi	2

it fitting that he should be buried close by, in a pavement tomb at the chapel entrance. (Another great artist, Verrocchio, who died in 1488, is buried in the fourth chapel.)

The narrative fresco (1486) alongside the tabernacle alludes to the miracle which gave the Cappella del Miracolo its name. The work of Cosimo Rosselli (best known for his frescoes in Santissima Annunziata), it depicts a procession bearing a chalice in which, during a Mass conducted here in 1230, the communion wine was discovered to have turned into blood. The Florentines believed the chalice saved them from, among other things, the effects of a plague outbreak of 1340. The painting is full of portraits of Rosselli's contemporaries, making it another of Florence's vivid pieces of Renaissance social reportage: Rosselli himself is the figure in the black beret at the extreme left of the picture.

The Synagogue

MAP PAGE 84, POCKET MAP G5
Via Farini 4. ⓦ jewishflorence.it. Charge.
The enormous domed building rising to the north of Sant'Ambrogio church is the **Synagogue**; the ghetto established in this district by Cosimo I was not demolished until the second half of the nineteenth century, which is when the present Moorish-style synagogue was built. It contains a **museum** that charts the history of Florence's Jewish population.

Santa Maria Maddalena dei Pazzi

MAP PAGE 84, POCKET MAP G4
Borgo Pinti. Free.
The church of **Santa Maria Maddalena dei Pazzi** is named after a Carmelite nun – a member of the clan who murdered Giuliano de' Medici – who was famed for her healing powers and religious ecstasies: when possessed by the spirit she would spew words at such a rate that a team of eight novices was needed to transcribe her inspired dictation. She was also prone to pouring boiling wax over her arms, and was fond of reclining naked on a bed of thorns. Such fervent piety was much honoured in Counter-Reformation Florence, and a cult grew up around her immediately after her death in 1607; canonisation followed in 1669.

Founded in the thirteenth century, the church is fronted by a lovely courtyard designed

The Synagogue

Le Murate

The former prison of Le Murate (ⓦ lemurate.comune.fi.it), at Piazza delle Murate in the Sant'Ambrogio district, is now a cultural centre, with two large halls and several smaller exhibition spaces. Box Office, the main outlet for concert and theatre tickets, has its main branch here, and there's a nice café as well.

by Giuliano da Sangallo. Inside, paintings celebrating St Maria – including a pair by Luca Giordano – adorn the marble-clad chancel. In contrast to all this Baroque fervour, the convent's chapterhouse – entered via a doorway at Via della Colonna 9 – is decorated with a radiant **Perugino** fresco of the *Crucifixion*. Based on the terrain around Lago Trasimeno, the scene is painted as a continuous panorama on a wall divided into three arches, giving the effect of looking out through a loggia onto a springtime landscape. As always with Perugino, there is nothing troubling here, the Crucifixion being depicted not as an agonizing death but rather as the necessary prelude to the Resurrection.

The English Cemetery

MAP PAGE 84, POCKET MAP H3
Piazza Donatello.

North of the Pazzi church, at the end of Borgo Pinti, lies the **English Cemetery**. Now stranded amid the traffic, this patch of garden is the resting place of Elizabeth Barrett Browning and a number of contemporary artistic Brits, among them Walter Savage Landor and Arthur Hugh Clough.

The Museo Horne

MAP PAGE 84, POCKET MAP F7
Via de' Benci 6 ⓦ museohorne.it. Charge.

On the south side of Santa Croce, not far from the river, stands one of Florence's more recondite museums, the **Museo della Fondazione Horne**. Its collection was left to the state by the English art historian Herbert Percy Horne (1864–1916), who was

instrumental in rescuing Botticelli from neglect with a pioneering biography that was published in 1908. The half-dozen rooms of paintings, sculptures, pottery, furniture and other domestic objects contain few masterpieces, but are diverting enough if you've already done the major collections.

The museum building, the fifteenth-century **Palazzo Corsi-Alberti**, is worth a look even if you're not going into the museum. Commissioned by the Corsi family, it's a typical merchant's house of the period, with huge cellars in which wool would have been dyed, and an open gallery above the courtyard for drying the finished cloth.

The pride of Horne's collection was its drawings, which are now salted away in the Uffizi, though a small selection is often displayed on the **ground floor**. On the first floor, Room 1 has pictures by Filippino Lippi and Piero di Cosimo, an unfinished and age-darkened *Deposition* by Gozzoli (his last documented work), a tiny and badly damaged panel by Masaccio, showing *Scenes from the Life of St Julian*, and a terracotta *Venus* by Giambologna. The next room contains the collection's big draw, Giotto's *St Stephen* (a fragment from a polyptych), which was probably painted at around the time Giotto was at work in Santa Croce. Room 3 has a tondo of the *Holy Family* by Beccafumi, who is also attributed with a *Drunkenness of Noah* on the **second floor**, where you'll find small works by Filippo and Filippino Lippi, and a portable diptych by Simone Martini and Lippo Memmi.

Shops & markets

Aquaflor

MAP PAGE 84, POCKET MAP F6
Borgo Santa Croce 6. ⓦ aquaflor.it.
Master perfumer Sileno Cheloni
has a "library" of some 1500
natural ingredients, gathered from
all over the world, with which to
create a range of fragrances that are
unique to this atelier. Off-the-peg
perfumes are €120–180 (bespoke
scents are much more), but soaps
start from €10.

Mercato di Sant'Ambrogio

MAP PAGE 84, POCKET MAP H5
Piazza Sant'Ambrogio.
Out of the orbit of most tourists,
the *Mercato di Sant'Ambrogio*
is a smaller, tattier but equally
enjoyable version of the San
Lorenzo food hall. The *tavola calda*
is one of Florence's lunchtime
bargains, and – as at San Lorenzo –
the stalls bring their prices down in
the last hour of trading.

Scuola del Cuoio

MAP PAGE 84, POCKET MAP G6
Via San Giuseppe 5r. ⓦ scuoladelcuoio.com.

Scuola del Cuoio

This academy for leather-workers
sells bags, jackets, belts and other
accessories at prices that compare
very favourably with the shops. You
won't find any startlingly original
designs here, but the quality is
very high and the staff are both
knowledgeable and helpful.

Gelaterie

Gelateria dei Neri

MAP PAGE 84, POCKET MAP F6
Via dei Neri 9–11r. ⓦ gelateriadeineri.it.
Located close to Santa Croce, *Dei
Neri* serves what many think is the
best ice cream in town. The range
of flavours is fantastic – fig and
walnut, Mexican chocolate (very
spicy), rice – and they have some
dairy-free ice cream too.

Vestri

MAP PAGE 84, POCKET MAP F5
Piazza Gaetano Salvemini 11r. ⓦ vestri.it.
Chocoholics should make a beeline
for *Vestri*, where ice cream is just
one of the concoctions on offer
– there's also deliciously thick
drinking chocolate and a mouth-
watering array of sweets and other
chocolate products. The ice cream
comes in a dozen flavours, but the
cocoa-based stuff is what they are
renowned for.

Vivoli

MAP PAGE 84, POCKET MAP F6
Via Isola delle Stinche 7r. ⓦ vivoli.it.
Operating from deceptively
ordinary premises in a side street
close to Santa Croce, this has long
been rated one of the best ice-
cream-makers in the city.

Cafés & bars

L'Antico Noè

MAP PAGE 84, POCKET MAP F5
Volta di San Piero 6r. ⓦ anticonoe.com.
The "Old Noah" is a long-
established and utterly authentic
stand-up wine bar, tucked into

Rex Caffè

an uninviting little alley to the
north of Santa Croce, at the
end of Borgo Albizi. Excellent
sandwiches and other snacks
available. €

Caffè Cibrèo

MAP PAGE 84, POCKET MAP G5
Via Andrea del Verrocchio 5r. Ⓦ cibreo.com.
Possibly the prettiest café in
Florence, with a chi-chi clientele to
match. Opened in 1989, the wood-
panelled interior looks at least two
hundred years older. Cakes and
desserts are great, and the light
meals bear the culinary stamp
of the *Cibrèo* restaurant kitchens
opposite. €

Ditta Artigianale

MAP PAGE 84, POCKET MAP D13
Via dei Neri 32. Ⓦ dittaartigianale.it.
The *Artigianale* has been in business
since 2013 and was the first coffee
shop to offer flat whites to the
citizens of Florence; some would
say it has the right to think of itself
as the city's coolest café. It might
be a bit too self-consciously hip
for some, but the coffee is terrific
– they showcase a different roast
every month. And it does look very

good – the architects who designed
the place were also responsible for
the spectacular *La Ménagère* (see
page 81). €

Moyo

MAP PAGE 84, POCKET MAP F6
Via de' Benci 23r. Ⓦ moyo.it.
A young crowd flocks to this bar
every evening – the food's pretty
good (come for the 6–10pm
aperitivo buffet), but it's the buzz
that really brings them in. There's a
DJ set on Monday, Wednesday and
Thursday, with everything from
Latin to hip-hop. €

Rex Caffè

MAP PAGE 84, POCKET MAP G5
Via Fiesolana 25r. Ⓦ rexfirenze.com.
One of the city's real night-time
fixtures, this is a friendly bar-club
with a varied and loyal clientele.
Vast curving lights droop over the
central bar, which is studded with
turquoise stone and broken mirror
mosaics. Big arched spaces to either
side mean there's plenty of room
for dancing the night away. The
cocktails are good and the snacks
excellent. DJs provide the sounds at
weekends.

Restaurants

L'Antico Noè

MAP PAGE 84, POCKET MAP F5

Volta di San Piero 8r. Ⓦ anticonoe.com.

Situated next door to the excellent *vinaio* of the same name (see page 49), this tiny and long-established trattoria is one for hard-core carnivores – plate-filling slabs of prime-quality grilled meat are the only *secondi* on offer. The décor is plain (you sit on wicker-seated stools), but the prices don't reflect the surroundings so much as the quality of the food – expect to pay upward of €25 for your steak. A popular spot for the cosy, rustic vibe and seasonal, fresh ingredients. €€

Cibrèo

MAP PAGE 84, POCKET MAP G5

Via de' Macci 118r. Ⓦ cibreo.com.

Fabio Picchi's restaurant is an obligatory port-of-call for many foodies, its creative take on Tuscan classics having achieved fame well beyond the city. Some think it's been resting on its laurels for too long, but many still rate it very highly. You'll need to book days in advance for a table in the main part of the restaurant, but next door there's a small, spartan and sometimes overly busy trattoria (*Cibreino*) where the food is virtually the same (though the menu is smaller), no bookings are taken and the prices are much lower. Picchi also opened the city's first Tuscan-Japanese-Korean fusion restaurant in 2017, a tiny place almost next door to *Cibrèo* at Via Verrocchio 2r called *Ciblèo*. €€

Enoteca Pinchiorri

MAP PAGE 84, POCKET MAP F6

Via Ghibellina 87. Ⓦ enotecapinchiorri.it.

This is the only Tuscan restaurant to have been given three Michelin stars, and no one seriously disputes *Pinchiorri's* claim to be Florence's best. The food is as magnificent as the plaudits suggest, but the formality of the place is not to everyone's taste. And the prices are delirious: pasta dishes can cost as much as €80, main courses around €100, while the ever-changing set menus cost from around €280 to €450 per person – though you may get as many as twenty exquisite little dishes in a *menu degustazione*. The wine list has no equal in Italy, with some 150,000 bottles lying in the *Pinchiorri* cellars; bottles start at about €100, rising to five-figure sums. €€€

Cibrèo

Osteria Caffè Italiano

MAP PAGE 84, POCKET MAP F6
Via Isola delle Stinche 11–13r.
Ⓦ caffeitaliano.it.

The vaulted and cabinet-lined front room of this upmarket café-wine bar-restaurant is one of the best-looking in Florence, and the food more than lives up to the setting. The cuisine is first-rate and typically Tuscan – lots of beef, veal and wild boar. In the evening, wood-oven pizzas are served in a small room next door. €€

La Pentola dell'Oro

MAP PAGE 84, POCKET MAP G5
Via di Mezzo 24r. Ⓦ lapentoladelloro.com.

La Pentola has one of the more imaginative menus in Florence, mingling the innovative with the profoundly traditional. Some of the recipes used by head chef Giuseppe Alessi date back as far as the fourteenth century, and there are three different types of *bistecca* on offer. Most main courses are reasonably priced considering the quality of the cooking, even if the basement dining room isn't the most comfortable in the city. €

Il Pizzaiuolo

MAP PAGE 84, POCKET MAP G5
Via de' Macci 113r. Ⓦ ilpizzaiuolo.it.

The recent boom in Neapolitan-style pizza restaurants in Florence has led to a huge choice for great pizza. One of the picks of the bunch is *Il Pizzaiuolo*, where the pizzas here are among the best in the city (there are thirty varieties on offer), and the rest of the menu has a Neapolitan touch too – as does the atmosphere. The wine list is full of southern Italian vintages rather than the usual Tuscans. Reservations advisable. €

Teatro del Sale

MAP PAGE 84, POCKET MAP G5
Via dei Macci 111r. Ⓦ teatrodelsale.com.

Run by Fabio Picchi, the boss of *Cibrèo* (see page 90), this unique place is a combination of restaurant and cultural centre. You pay an annual membership fee which includes one guest, and then an extra amount to help yourself to the amazing buffets: prices vary depending on whether you want breakfast, lunch, or dinner, as well as brunch on Saturdays. Dinner is especially fabulous because Picchi himself is often on duty in the open kitchen, announcing the dishes as they're put out. Just before 10pm, guests are treated to a show, which might be anything from stand-up comedy to a piano recital or a dance group. If you don't want to eat, you can just hang out, drink coffee and browse through the books and magazines that are lying around. Needless to say, it's very popular, and reservations are advisable in the evenings. €€

Theatre & classical music

Teatro della Pergola

MAP PAGE 84, POCKET MAP F5
Via della Pergola 18.
Ⓦ teatrodellapergola.com.

The beautiful little Pergola was built in 1656 and is Italy's oldest surviving theatre. It plays host to top-flight instrumental recitals, chamber concerts and some of the best-known Italian theatre companies. The theatre season runs from October to April, and during the Maggio Musicale the Pergola is often used for small-scale operas.

Teatro Verdi

MAP PAGE 84, POCKET MAP F6
Via Ghibellina 99–101.
Ⓦ teatroverdifirenze.it.

Home to the Orchestra della Toscana, *Teatro Verdi* is one of the city's premier venues for classical music, musicals and mainstream theatre productions. It hosts rock bands occasionally too.

Oltrarno

The artisanal quarter of the city, the Oltrarno – literally "beyond the Arno" – contains several of the city's key sights. The biggest of these, Palazzo Pitti, is a colossal palace whose cluster of museums includes the city's second-ranking picture gallery, and whose garden, the Giardino di Bóboli, is Italy's most visited. Close by, the main church of Oltrarno, Santo Spirito, overlooks a piazza that typifies the gentrification that's happening in some parts of this quarter. From Santo Spirito it's a brief stroll to Santa Maria del Carmine, where the Cappella Brancacci contains an epoch-defining fresco cycle. On the other side of Oltrarno, the medieval Via dei Bardi and its continuation, Via San Niccolò, take you past the engagingly eclectic Museo Bardini, which you can visit en route to the Romanesque gem of San Miniato al Monte. Other major sights include Santa Felìcita and the extraordinary waxworks of La Specola. And on top of all this, there's a greater concentration of good bars and restaurants here than in any other part of Florence – indeed, the Piazza Santo Spirito area has become so popular with tourists that it's known to some locals as "Santo Spiritoland", just as the equivalent on the other side of the river has been dubbed "Santa Croceland".

Ponte Vecchio

MAP PAGE 94, POCKET MAP B13

The direct route from the city centre to the heart of the Oltrarno crosses the Arno via the **Ponte Vecchio**, the "old bridge". Until 1218 the crossing here was the city's only bridge, though the version you see today dates from 1345, built to replace a wooden bridge swept away by floods twelve years earlier. The Ponte Vecchio has always been loaded with shops like those now propped over the water. Their earliest tenants were butchers and fishmongers, attracted to the site by the proximity of the river, which provided a convenient dumping ground for their waste. The current plethora of jewellers dates from 1593, when Ferdinando

I evicted the butchers' stalls and other practitioners of what he called "vile arts". In their place he installed eight jewellers and 41 goldsmiths, also taking the opportunity to double the rents. Florence had long revered the art of the goldsmith, and several of its major artists were skilled in the craft: Ghiberti, Donatello and Cellini, for example. The third of this trio is celebrated by a bust in the centre of the bridge.

Santa Felìcita

MAP PAGE 94, POCKET MAP D7

Piazza Santa Felìcita. Free.

Some claim that **Santa Felìcita** has an even longer lineage than San Lorenzo (see page 66), and that a church was founded here in the second century by Greek or Syrian merchants. What's known for certain is that a church existed on this site by the fifth century, by which time it had been dedicated to St Felicity; new churches were built in the eleventh and fourteenth centuries, then in 1565 Vasari added an elaborate portico to accommodate the *corridoio* linking the Uffizi and Palazzo Pitti; a window from the corridor looks directly into the church.

The interior demands a visit for the amazing Pontormo paintings in the **Cappella Capponi**, which lies to the right of the main door, surrounded by obstructive railings. The chapel was designed in the 1420s by Brunelleschi, but subsequently much altered – notably by Vasari, who destroyed the Pontormo fresco in the cupola when building his corridor. Under the cupola are four tondi of the Evangelists (painted with help from Pontormo's adoptive son, Bronzino), while on opposite sides of the window on the right wall are the Virgin and the angel of Pontormo's delightfully simple *Annunciation*. The low level of

light admitted by this window was a determining factor in the startling colour scheme of the painter's *Deposition* (1525–28), one of the masterworks of Florentine Mannerism. Nothing in this picture is conventional: Mary is on a different scale from her attendants; the figures bearing Christ's body are androgynous beings clad in acidic sky-blue, puce green and candy-floss pink drapery; and there's no sign of the Cross, the thieves, or any of the other scene-setting devices usual in paintings of this subject.

Palazzo Pitti

MAP PAGE 94, POCKET MAP C7–D7
Piazza Pitti. ◎ bit.ly/PittiPalazzo. Charge, joint ticket with other sights available.
Beyond Santa Felìcita, the street opens out at Piazza Pitti, forecourt of the largest palace in Florence, the **Palazzo Pitti**. Banker and merchant Luca Pitti commissioned the palace in the 1450s to outdo his rivals, the Medici, but in 1549 the cash-strapped Pitti were forced to sell out – to the Medici. This subsequently became the Medicis' base in Florence, growing in bulk

Ponte Vecchio

Florence's brief tenure as the Italian capital between 1865 and 1871, it housed the Italian kings.

Today the Palazzo Pitti and the pavilions of the Giardino di Bóboli contain eight museums, of which the foremost is the **Galleria Palatina**, an art collection second in importance only to the Uffizi. The Palatina possesses superb works by Fra' Bartolomeo, Filippo and Filippino Lippi, Caravaggio, Rosso Fiorentino and Canova, no fewer than seventeen pieces by Andrea del Sarto, and numerous paintings by **Raphael** and **Titian**.

When Raphael settled in Florence in 1505, he was besieged with commissions from patrons delighted to find an artist for whom the creative process involved so little agonizing. Among the masterpieces on show here are Raphael's portraits of Angelo Doni and his wife, Maddalena, and the wonderful

The Palazzo Pitti

until the seventeenth century, when it achieved its present gargantuan dimensions. Later, during

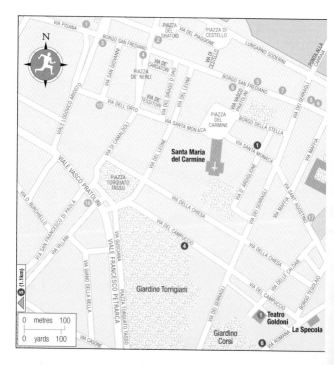

Madonna della Seggiola (Madonna of the Chair), which was once Italy's most popular image of the Madonna – nineteenth-century copyists had to join a five-year waiting list to study the picture. According to Vasari, the model for the famous *Donna Velata* (Veiled Woman), in the Sala di Giove, was the painter's mistress, a Roman baker's daughter known to posterity as La Fornarina.

The paintings by Titian include a number of his most trenchant portraits. The lecherous and scurrilous Pietro Aretino – journalist, critic, poet and one of Titian's closest friends – was so thrilled by his portrait that he gave it to Cosimo I. Also here are likenesses of Philip II of Spain and the young Cardinal Ippolito de' Medici, also the so-called *Portrait of an Englishman*, who scrutinizes the viewer with unflinching sea-grey eyes. To his left, by way of contrast, is the same artist's sensuous and much-copied *Mary Magdalene*, the first of a series on this theme produced for the Duke of Urbino. In the same room, look out for the gallery's outstanding sculpture, Canova's *Venus Italica*, commissioned by Napoleon as a replacement for the *Venus de' Medici*, which he had whisked off to Paris.

Much of the rest of the Pitti's first floor comprises the **Appartamenti Reali**, the Pitti's state rooms; after Raphael and Titian it can be difficult to sustain a great deal of enthusiasm for such ducal elegance, notwithstanding the sumptuousness of the furnishings.

On the floor above the Palatina is the **Galleria d'Arte Moderna**, which comprises a chronological survey of primarily Tuscan art from the mid-eighteenth century to 1945. Much space is devoted

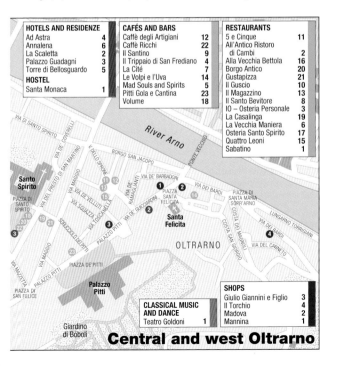

HOTELS AND RESIDENZE	
Ad Astra	4
Annalena	6
La Scaletta	2
Palazzo Guadagni	3
Torre di Bellosguardo	5
HOSTEL	
Santa Monaca	1

CAFÉS AND BARS	
Caffè degli Artigiani	12
Caffè Ricchi	22
Il Santino	9
Il Trippaio di San Frediano	4
La Cité	7
Le Volpi e l'Uva	14
Mad Souls and Spirits	5
Pitti Gola e Cantina	23
Volume	18

RESTAURANTS	
5 e Cinque	11
All'Antico Ristoro di Cambi	2
Alla Vecchia Bettola	16
Borgo Antico	20
Gustapizza	21
Il Guscio	10
Il Magazzino	13
Il Santo Bevitore	8
IO – Osteria Personale	3
La Casalinga	19
La Vecchia Maniera	6
Osteria Santo Spirito	17
Quattro Leoni	15
Sabatino	1

CLASSICAL MUSIC AND DANCE	
Teatro Goldoni	1

SHOPS	
Giulio Giannini e Figlio	3
Il Torchio	4
Madova	2
Mannina	1

Central and west Oltrarno

to the work of the Macchiaioli (the open-air painters who were in some respects the Italian equivalent of the Impressionists), but there's a lot of mediocre stuff here, with ranks of academically proficient portraits, bombastic history paintings and sentimental dross such as Rodolfo Morgari's *Raphael Dying* and Gabriele Castagnola's depiction of Fra' Filippo Lippi on the brink of kissing the lovely young novice, Lucrezia Buti.

The **Tesoro dei Granduchi**, entered from the main palace courtyard, is a colossal museum not just of silverware but of luxury artefacts acquired by the Medici. The craftsmanship on show is astounding, even if the final products are likely to strike you as being in dubious taste – room after room is packed with seashell figurines, cups made from ostrich eggs, portraits in stone inlay, bizarre ivory carvings, and the like. Amid all the trinkets, look out for the death mask of Lorenzo il Magnifico.

Finally, in the Palazzina della Meridiana, the eighteenth-century southern wing of the Pitti, the **Galleria del Costume** provides the opportunity to see the dress that Eleonora di Toledo was buried in (it's the one she's wearing in Bronzino's portrait of her in the Palazzo Vecchio).

The Giardino di Bóboli

MAP PAGE 94, POCKET MAP B9–D7
ⓦ bit.ly/BoboliGarden. Charge, joint ticket with other sights available.

The land occupied by the formal gardens of the Palazzo Pitti, the **Giardino di Bóboli**, was once a quarry; the bedrock here is one of the sources of the yellow sandstone known as *pietra forte* (strong stone) that gives much of Florence its dominant hue. When the Medici acquired the house they set about transforming their backyard into an enormous garden, its every statue, view and grotto designed to elevate nature by the judicious application of art. The resulting landscape takes its name from the **Bóboli family**, erstwhile owners of some of the land. Opened to the public in 1766, this is the only really extensive area of accessible greenery in the centre of the city. It attracts some five million visitors annually, more than any other Italian garden.

Of all the garden's Mannerist embellishments, the most celebrated is the **Grotta del Buontalenti** (1583–88), to the left of the entrance, beyond Giambologna's much-reproduced statue of Cosimo I's favourite dwarf astride a giant tortoise. Embedded in the grotto's faked stalactites and encrustations are replicas of Michelangelo's *Slaves* – the originals were lodged here until 1908. Lurking in the deepest recesses of the cave, and normally viewable only from afar, is Giambologna's *Venus Emerging from her Bath*, leered at by attendant imps.

Another spectacular set-piece is the fountain island called the **Isolotto**, which is the focal point

The Forte di Belvedere

The Forte di Belvedere, the fortress that overlooks the back of the Pitti, was built by Buontalenti on the orders of Ferdinando I between 1590 and 1595, ostensibly to protect the city, but in fact to intimidate the grand duke's subjects. The urban panorama from here is superb, but the Belvedere is open only when exhibitions are being held in and around the shed-like palace in the centre of the fortress.

Giardino di Bóboli

of the far end of the garden;
from within the Bóboli the most
dramatic approach is along the
central cypress avenue known as the
Viottolone, many of whose statues
are Roman originals.

La Specola

MAP PAGE 94, POCKET MAP C8
Via Romana 17. ⓦ bit.ly/SpecolaMuseum.
On the third floor of the
university buildings on Via
Romana there lurks what can
reasonably claim to be the
strangest museum in the city.
Taking its name from the
telescope (*specola*) on its roof,
La Specola is a twin-sectioned
**museum of zoology and
natural history**. The first part is
conventional enough, with ranks
of shells, insects and crustaceans,
followed by a mortician's ark
of animals stuffed, pickled and
desiccated. Beyond some rather
frayed-looking sharks lie the
things everyone comes to see, the
Cere Anatomiche (Anatomical
Waxworks). Wax arms, legs and
organs cover the walls, arrayed
around satin beds on which wax

cadavers recline in progressive
stages of deconstruction, each
muscle fibre and nerve cluster
moulded and dyed with absolute
precision. Most of the six hundred
models were made between 1775
and 1791 by Clemente Susini,
and were intended as teaching
aids, in an age when medical
ethics and refrigeration techniques
were not what they are today.

The grisliest section of La Specola
consists of a trio of tableaux
that were moulded in the late
seventeenth century by **Gaetano
Zumbo**, a cleric from Sicily who
was one of the pioneers of the art
of anatomical waxwork. Whereas
Susini's masterpieces were created
to educate, these were made to
horrify, and to horrify one man in
particular: the hypochondriacal
Cosimo III. Enclosed in tasteful
display cabinets, they depict
Florence during the plague, with
rats teasing the intestines from
rotting corpses, and the pink bodies
of the freshly dead heaped on the
suppurating semi-decomposed.
A fourth tableau, illustrating the
horrors of syphilis, was damaged

Wax cadaver in La Specola

in the 1966 flood, and now consists of a loose gathering of the deceased and diseased. Alongside is displayed a dissected waxwork head, built on the foundation of a real skull; it's as fastidious as any of Susini's creations, but Zumbo couldn't resist giving the skin a tint of putrefaction, before applying a dribble of blood to the mouth and nose.

This site closed in 2019 for renovations and was due to reopen in 2023, but as often happens in Italy, the date seems to be continually pushed back. It is worth checking the current situation before you visit.

Santo Spirito

MAP PAGE 94, POCKET MAP C7
Piazza Santa Spirito.
Ⓦ basilicasantospirito.it. Free, charge for some exhibits and events.

Designed in 1434 as a replacement for a thirteenth-century church, **Santo Spirito** was one of Brunelleschi's last projects, a swansong later described by Bernini as "the most beautiful church in

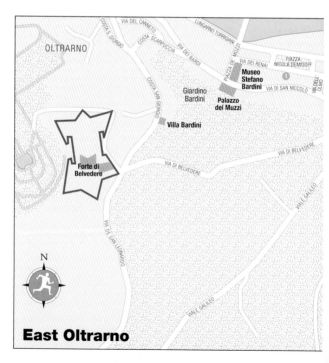

OLTRARNO

VIA DEL CANNETO
COSTA S. GIORGIO
COSTA SCARPUCCIA
VIA DE' BARDI
LUNGARNO TORRIGIANI
VIA DEI RENAI
PIAZZA NICOLA DEMIDOFF
PIAZZA DE' MOZZI

Museo Stefano Bardini
VIA DI SAN NICCOLÒ
VIA DELL' OLMO

COSTA SAN GIORGIO

Giardino Bardini
Palazzo dei Muzzi

Villa Bardini

VIA DI BELVEDERE

Forte di Belvedere

VIA DI BELVEDERE

VIALE GALILEO

VIA DI SAN LEONARDO

N

VIALE GALILEO

East Oltrarno

the world". Its plan is extremely sophisticated: a Latin cross with a continuous chain of 38 chapels round the outside and a line of 35 columns running without a break round the nave, transepts and chancel. The exterior wall was designed to follow the curves of the chapels' walls; as built, however, the exterior is plain and straight, and the facade was never completed. Inside, only the Baroque baldachin disrupts the harmony of Brunelleschi's design.

A fire in 1471 destroyed most of Santo Spirito's medieval works, including frescoes by Cimabue and the Gaddi family, but as a result the altar paintings comprise an unusually unified collection of religious works, the majority having been commissioned in the aftermath of the fire. Most prolific among the artists is the so-called **Maestro di Santo Spirito**, but the finest single painting is

Filippino Lippi's *Nerli Altarpiece* (c.1488), an age-darkened Madonna and Child with saints, which hangs in the south transept. A door in the north aisle leads through to Giuliano da Sangallo's stunning vestibule and **sacristy** (1489–93), the latter designed in imitation of Brunelleschi's Cappella dei Pazzi. Hanging above the altar is a delicate wooden crucifix attributed to the young Michelangelo.

The 1471 fire destroyed much of the rest of the monastery, with the exception of its refectory (entered to the left of the main church), which is now the home of the **Fondazione Salvatore Romano** (charge, joint ticket available with Cappella Brancacci), a one-room collection comprising an assortment of carvings, many of them Romanesque, and a huge fresco of *The Crucifixion* (1365) by Orcagna and his workshop.

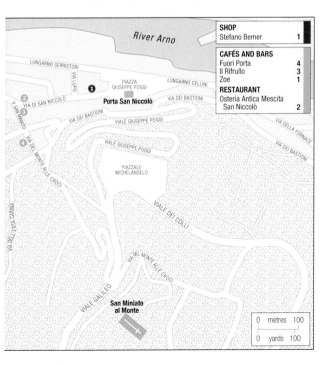

SHOP	
Stefano Bemer	1

CAFÉS AND BARS	
Fuori Porta	4
Il Rifrullo	3
Zoe	1

RESTAURANT	
Osteria Antica Mescita San Niccolò	2

The Cappella Brancacci, Santa Maria del Carmine

The Cappella Brancacci

MAP PAGE 94, POCKET MAP B6
Piazza del Carmine. ⓦ bit.ly/CappellaB.
Charge, reservations recommended.

In 1771 **fire** wrecked the Carmelite convent and church of Santa Maria del Carmine some 300m west of Santo Spirito, but somehow the flames did not damage the frescoes of the church's **Cappella Brancacci**, a cycle of paintings that is one of the essential sights of Florence. The chapel is barricaded off from the rest of the Carmine, and visits are restricted to a maximum of ten people at a time for thirty minutes.

The decoration of the chapel was begun in 1424 by **Masolino** and **Masaccio**, when the former was aged 41 and the latter just 22. Within a short time the elder was taking lessons from the younger, whose grasp of the texture of the real world, of the principles of perspective, and of the dramatic potential of the biblical texts they were illustrating far exceeded that of his precursors. In 1428 Masolino was called away to Rome, where he was followed by Masaccio a few months later. Neither would return to the chapel. Masaccio died the same year, aged just 27, but, in the words of Vasari, "All the most celebrated sculptors and painters since Masaccio's day have become excellent and illustrious by studying their art in this chapel."

The Brancacci frescoes are as startling as the Sistine Chapel in Rome, the brightness and delicacy of their colours and the solidity of the figures exemplifying what Bernard Berenson singled out as the tactile quality of Florentine art. The small scene on the left of the entrance arch is the quintessence of Masaccio's art. Depictions of **The Expulsion of Adam and Eve** had never before captured the desolation of the sinners so graphically – Adam presses his hands to his face in bottomless despair, Eve raises her head and screams. In contrast, Masolino's dainty *Adam and Eve*, opposite, pose as if to have their portraits painted.

St Peter is chief protagonist of most of the remaining scenes, some of which were left unfinished in 1428 – work did not resume until 1480, when the frescoes were completed by **Filippino Lippi**. One of the scenes finished by Lippi is the *Raising of Theophilus's Son and St Peter Enthroned*, which depicts St Peter bringing the son of the Prefect of Antioch to life and then preaching to the people of the city. The three figures to the right of his throne are thought to be Masaccio, Alberti and Brunelleschi.

The Museo Stefano Bardini

MAP PAGE 98, POCKET MAP E7
Piazza de' Mozzi 1. ⓦ bit.ly/StefanoBardini.
Charge.

The **Museo Stefano Bardini**, which stands at the end of the handsome Via de' Bardi, houses the collection of **Stefano Bardini** (1836–1922), once the most important art dealer in Italy, whose tireless activity laid the cornerstone of many important European and American museums. Determined that no visitor to his native city should remain unaware of his success, he bought the former monastery of San Gregorio alla Pace, and converted it into a vast house for himself and his collection. Sculpture, paintings, ceramics, armour, furniture, picture frames, carpets, wooden ceilings, tombstones – Bardini bought it all, and he bequeathed the whole lot to the city. Reopened in 2011 after a protracted restoration, the museum now looks much as it did when Bardini died, though a few pieces – notably Pietro Tacca's bronze boar and Giambologna's so-called *Diavolino* (Little Devil) – were added after his death.

The Bardini is more like a colossal **showroom** than a modern museum, with miscellaneous unlabelled objets d'art strewn all about the place, often following their owner's personal logic. The most interesting items are **upstairs**, where you'll find two reliefs of the *Madonna and Child* that may be by Donatello (in a room that's stacked with similar reliefs), a beautiful terracotta *Virgin Annunciate* from fifteenth-century Siena, and some fine drawings by Giambattista Tiepolo and his son Lorenzo. Most of the paintings are unremarkable, but there are exceptions, notably Guercino's *Atlas*, Michele Giambono's *St John the Evangelist*, and a *St Michael* by Antonio del Pollaiuolo. The main staircase is hung with gorgeous carpets, the largest of which was damaged by Hitler's spurs when it was laid out to welcome the Führer at Santa Maria Novella station.

Giardino Bardini

MAP PAGE 98, POCKET MAP E8
Entrances at Costa di San Giorgio 2 and Via de' Bardi 1r. ⓦ villabardini.it. Charge, joint ticket available with Giardino di Bóboli.

The **Giardino Bardini** occupies the slope that was formerly the olive grove of the **Palazzo dei Mozzi**, a colossal house built in the late

Museo Stefano Bardini

thirteenth century by the Mozzi family, at that time one of the richest families in Florence. (The palazzo houses a collection of seven hundred paintings donated to the city in 1937 by Fortunata Carobbi Corsi; there's a plan to put them on public show.)

After Stefano Bardini bought the property in 1913 he set about creating a semi-formal garden which has now been restored to the appearance he gave it, with a neo-Baroque staircase and terraces dividing the fruit-growing section from the miniature woodland of the "*bosco inglese*". At the summit of the garden, reached by a lovely long pergola of wisteria and hortensia, a colonnaded belvedere gives a splendid view of the city.

Villa Bardini

MAP PAGE 98, POCKET MAP E8
Costa di San Giorgio 2. Ⓦ villabardini.it. Charge, joint ticket available with Giardino di Bóboli.

At the top of the Giardino Bardini stands the **Villa Bardini**, built in the seventeenth century and extended by Stefano Bardini. Having been thoroughly

Giardino Bardini

restored, the villa is used as an exhibition space and also houses a museum dedicated to **Pietro Annigoni** (1910–88), a vehemently anti-Modernist painter who was best known for his portraits of luminaries such as Pope John XXIII and Queen Elizabeth II. Fashionistas may enjoy the villa's collection of clothes created by Roberto Capucci (born 1930). Dubbed the "Givenchy of Rome" by his admirers, Capucci made his name with frocks that seemed intent on upstaging their wearer – one of his most celebrated creations was a nine-layered dress that became famous when worn by a model in Cadillac ads in the 1950s. One-off exhibitions at the Bardini are held on the third floor, and are usually free; the third floor has another attraction – a belvedere that gives you a glorious view of the city.

The city gates and Piazzale Michelangelo

MAP PAGE 98, POCKET MAP G8
In medieval times San Niccolò was close to the edge of the city, and two of Florence's fourteenth-century gates still stand in the vicinity: the diminutive **Porta San Miniato**, set in a portion of the walls, and the huge **Porta San Niccolò**, overlooking the Arno. From either of these gates you can begin the climb up to San Miniato: the path from Porta San Niccolò weaves up through **Piazzale Michelangelo**, with its replica *David* and fine views; the more direct path from Porta San Miniato leads to the stepped Via di San Salvatore al Monte, which emerges a short distance uphill from Piazzale Michelangelo.

San Miniato al Monte

MAP PAGE 98, POCKET MAP G9
Via del Monte alle Croci. Free.
Perhaps the finest Romanesque structure in Tuscany, **San Miniato al Monte** is also the oldest

San Miniato al Monte

sacred building in Florence after the Baptistery. The dedicatee is **St Minias**, Florence's first home-grown martyr. Legend has it that after decapitation in the centre of the city, the saintly corpse was seen to carry his severed head up the hill to this spot. A chapel devoted to Minias was built here in the eighth century, though construction of the present building began in 1013. Initially a Benedictine foundation, since 1373 it has belonged to the Olivetans, a Benedictine offshoot.

The lower part of the gorgeous marble facade is possibly eleventh-century, while the upper levels date from the twelfth century onwards, and were financed in part by the Arte di Calimala (cloth merchants' guild): their trademark, an eagle clutching a bale of cloth, perches up top.

The floor of the sublime **interior** is adorned by an elaborately patterned pavement that's dated 1207, while the middle of the nave is dominated by the lovely tabernacle designed in 1448 by Michelozzo. Steps either side of the tabernacle lead down to

the **crypt**, where the original high altar contains the alleged bones of St Minias. Above, the **choir** and **presbytery** have a magnificent Romanesque pulpit and screen, and a great mosaic of *Christ Pantocrator*, created in 1297. Off the presbytery lies the **sacristy** (charge), whose walls are covered in a superlative fresco cycle by Spinello Aretino (1387), illustrating the life of St Benedict.

Back in the lower body of the church, off the left side of the nave, the **Cappella del Cardinale del Portogallo** constitutes one of Renaissance Florence's supreme examples of artistic collaboration. Completed in 1473, it was designed by Antonio di Manetto, a pupil and biographer of Brunelleschi, while the tomb was carved by Antonio and Bernardo Rossellino. The carefully integrated frescoes and paintings are by Alesso Baldovinetti, but Antonio and Piero del Pollaiuolo produced the main altarpiece (this is a copy, the original being in the Uffizi). The ceiling's tiled decoration and four glazed terracotta medallions were provided by Luca della Robbia.

Shops

Giulio Giannini e Figlio

MAP PAGE 94, POCKET MAP C7
Piazza Pitti 36r. Ⓦ giuliogiannini.it.
Established in 1856, this paper-
making and book-binding firm has
been honoured with exhibitions
dedicated to its work. Once the
only place in Florence to make its
own marbled papers, it now also
offers a wide variety of diaries,
address books and so forth.

Madova

MAP PAGE 94, POCKET MAP D7
Via Guicciardini 1r. Ⓦ madova.com.
The last word in gloves – every
colour, every size, every style, lined
with lambswool, silk, cashmere or
nothing. Prices range from around
€50 to €200.

Mannina

MAP PAGE 94, POCKET MAP D7
Via Guicciardini 16r.
Ⓦ manninafirenze.com.

This famed Oltrarno shoemaker has
been going since the 1950s, when it
was founded by Calogero Mannina,
father of the current boss, Antonio.
He produces beautifully made and
sensible footwear at prices that are
far from extravagant – many styles
under €200 for women and €400
for men.

Stefano Bemer

MAP PAGE 98, POCKET MAP G8
Via San Niccolò 2. Ⓦ stefanobemer.com.
If you're in the market for made-
to-measure Italian shoes of the
very highest quality, there's no
better place than this – prior to his
premature death in 2012, Stefano
Bemer was revered as perhaps
Italy's finest shoemaker, and his
apprentices continue to produce
footwear to Stefano's demanding
standards. The shop also sells
Bemer'S [sic], the off-the-peg (but
still expensive) footwear designed
by Stefano and his brother Mario,
who are committed to creating
high-quality products.

Gloves for sale in Madova

Il Torchio

MAP PAGE 94, POCKET MAP E7
Via de' Bardi 17. ⓦ legatoriailtorchio.com.
Founded in 1980 and now owned
by young Sicilian-Canadian Erin
Ciulla, *Il Torchio* produces marbled
paper, desk accessories, diaries,
albums and other items in paper
and leather.

Cafés & bars

Caffè degli Artigiani

MAP PAGE 94, POCKET MAP D7
Via dello Sprone 16r. ⓦ facebook.com/
caffedegliartigiani.
This cute little bar-café in the
corner of Piazza Passera is an
excellent spot for a recuperative
coffee or spritz after a tour of the
Pitti palace. Nice cakes too, and the
menu has some interesting salads
for a light lunch. €

Caffè Ricchi

MAP PAGE 94, POCKET MAP C7
Piazza di Santo Spirito 9r.
ⓦ ristorantericchi.com.
In business since 1957, this is
the oldest and the smartest of the
café-bars on this square, with a
good selection of cakes, ice cream
and lunchtime snacks, and superb
coffee. €

La Cité

MAP PAGE 94, POCKET MAP B6
Borgo San Frediano 20r.
ⓦ lacitelibreria.info.
With its huge windows, mezzanine
balcony and shelves of books (to
buy or just to browse), this café-
bar-bookshop has an arty, quasi-
Parisian ambience. An area is set
aside for live performances (usually
music). €

Fuori Porta

MAP PAGE 98, POCKET MAP F8
Via del Monte alle Croci 10r.
ⓦ fuoriporta.it.
If you're climbing up to San
Miniato, you could take a breather
at this justly famous wine bar-

osteria. There are over four hundred
wines to choose from by the bottle,
and an ever-changing selection by
the glass, as well as a wide selection
of grappas and malt whiskies.
Bread, cheese, ham and salami are
available, together with a choice of
pasta dishes and tasty *secondi*. €

Mad Souls and Spirits

MAP PAGE 94, POCKET MAP B6
Borgo S. Frediano 36/38r.
ⓦ madsoulsandspirits.com.
The self-proclaimed 'awesomest'
cocktail bar in Europe does a lot to
live up to the hype! This place has
a laid-back atmosphere and a dive-
bar feel, with a quirky interior and
friendly bartenders making creative
cocktails from a regularly changing
menu. €

Pitti Gola e Cantina

MAP PAGE 94, POCKET MAP C7
Piazza Pitti 16. ⓦ pittigolaecantina.com.
Small and friendly wine bar, run
by knowledgeable people; the
food – mainly cold meats and
handmade pasta – is very good.
€€

Il Rifrullo

MAP PAGE 98, POCKET MAP F8
Via San Niccolò 53–57r. ⓦ ilrifrullo.com.
Lying to the east of the Ponte
Vecchio–Pitti Palace route, this
place attracts fewer tourists than
many Oltrarno café-bars. Delicious
snacks with the early-evening
aperitivi (when the music gets
turned up), as well as more
substantial (and quite pricey) dishes
in the restaurant section. There's a
pleasant garden terrace too. €€

Il Santino

MAP PAGE 94, POCKET MAP C6
Via Santo Spirito 60r.
ⓦ facebook.com/ilsantinofi.
This small gastronomic *alimentari*-
cum-wine bar is an offshoot of the
neighbouring *Il Santo Bevitore* (see
page 107), and is proving just as
successful. The wines on offer are
top quality, as are the snacks. €

Il Trippaio di San Frediano

MAP PAGE 94. POCKET MAP A6
Piazza dei Nerli.

A bun filled with tripe or
lampredotto (deluxe tripe), slathered
in spicy sauce, is the quintessential
Florentine snack. If you want to
give it a try, this stall is the place.
For the less adventurous there
are burgers and hot dogs. Similar
stalls can be found by the Mercato
Nuovo, in Piazza dei Cimatori
(just to the north of Piazza della
Signora), and near to *Cibrèo*, in Via
dei Macci. €

Le Volpi e l'Uva

MAP PAGE 94, POCKET MAP D7
Piazza dei Rossi 1r. ⓦ levolpieluva.com.

This discreet, friendly little
enoteca does good business by
concentrating on the wines of small
producers and providing tasty cold
meats and snacks (the selection of
cheeses is tremendous). At any one
time you can choose from at least
two dozen different wines by the
glass. €

Volume

MAP PAGE 94, POCKET MAP C7
Piazza Santo Spirito 5r.
ⓦ volumefirenze.com.

This is the most idiosyncratic
of the bar-cafés on Piazza Santo
Spirito – it used to be a workshop
used by makers of hat forms,
and the walls of the front room
are still hung with the tools of
the trade. Art works and craft
items are on display in the cosy
back room, along with books
(*Volume* markets itself as "il caffè
culturale"), and there's often live
music in the evening – otherwise,
expect a DJ. It's invariably busy,
as are its neighbours, *Cabiria* and
Popcafè. €

Zoe

MAP PAGE 98, POCKET MAP F7
Via dei Renai 13. ⓦ zoebar.it.

Zoe is perennially popular for
summer evening drinks, but also
attracts lots of young Florentines
right through the day. Breakfast is
served from 8am–noon, lunch from

Neapolitan pizzas, the speciality at *Gustapizza*

noon–4pm, then it's "Aperitif" from 5–10pm (the Crimson Zoe cocktail is notorious), before the DJ gets the partying started. It also does good snacks and simple meals, and it's something of an art venue too. €

Restaurants

5 e Cinque

MAP PAGE 94, POCKET MAP C7
Piazza della Passera 1. Ⓦ 5ecinque.it.
This busy little café-restaurant on the iconic Piazza della Passera is one of the city's rare havens for vegetarians and never disappoints – dishes made from organic vegetables are the focus, and the wines are organic too. It's more a place for a quick and light meal than a lingering evening, but the food from the Ligurian menu is good and the staff very warm. €

All'Antico Ristoro di Cambi

MAP PAGE 94, POCKET MAP A6
Via Sant'Onofrio 1r.
Ⓦ anticoristorodicambi.it.
Run by the same family since the 1940s, this big, efficient yet homely trattoria is particularly good for meaty Florentine standards such as wild boar and steak, and has a fine wine list. It's vast, but nonetheless gets packed on a Saturday night, when even the large terrace fills up with a mixture of locals and visitors. €€

Alla Vecchia Bettola

MAP PAGE 94, POCKET MAP A7
Viale Vasco Pratolini 3–7. Ⓣ 055 224 158.
Located on a major traffic intersection a couple of minutes' walk from the Carmine, this wonderfully old-fashioned place – with its marble-topped tables – has something of the atmosphere of an old-style drinking den, which is what it once was; it boasts a good repertoire of Tuscan meat dishes. Long communal tables foster a convivial atmosphere. €€

Borgo Antico

MAP PAGE 94, POCKET MAP C7
Piazza di Santo Spirito 6r.
Ⓦ borgoanticofirenze.com.
With its smartly unfussy decor of white tiles and ochre plasterwork, the *Borgo Antico* reflects the increasingly trendy character of this once notoriously sleazy Oltrarno piazza. In summer the outside tables here are invariably packed, and the majority of the clientele are usually foreigners. But *Borgo Antico* is not one of Florence's cynical tourist-traps: the food (pizza, plus Tuscan standards) is generally good, prices are fair, and the servings are generous to a fault. €€

Gustapizza

MAP PAGE 94, POCKET MAP C7
Via Maggio 46r. Ⓦ facebook.com/GustapizzaFirenze.
The wood-fired Neapolitan pizzas are all they serve here, which is always a good thing, and they're the best in Oltrarno. It's cheap, busy and basic, and no reservations are taken, so be prepared to queue. €

Il Guscio

MAP PAGE 94, POCKET MAP A6
Via dell'Orto 49. Ⓦ ristorante-ilguscio.it.
This smart rustic-style restaurant is a long-established Oltrano favourite: high-quality Tuscan meat and fish dishes, superb desserts and a wide-ranging wine list, and it's not that expensive. €€

Il Magazzino

MAP PAGE 94, POCKET MAP C7
Piazza della Passera 2–3. Ⓣ 055 215 969.
Occupying a corner of the very lively little Piazza Passera, *Il Magazzino* is an earthily authentic but high-class *osteria-tripperia*, serving hearty dishes of pasta, tripe and beef. Dishes range from classic to creative with plenty of choice for non-tripe eaters. €€

Il Santo Bevitore

MAP PAGE 94, POCKET MAP C6

Via Santo Spirito 64–66r.
🌐 ilsantobevitore.com.

"The Holy Drinker" is an airy, stylish and hugely popular gastronomic *enoteca* with a small but classy menu of seasonal food to complement its enticing wine list. Very busy throughout the year, especially in the evenings, so you'd best book a table. The platters of cold meats and cheese make an excellent lunch. €€

Io – Osteria Personale

MAP PAGE 94, POCKET MAP A6
Borgo San Frediano 167r. 🌐 io-osteriapersonale.it.

Run by a young and imaginative team, this is one of the very best restaurants in Florence in recent years. The minimalist decor – bare brick walls and very upright chairs – send out the message that this place is serious about its food, and not just another purveyor of routine Tuscan recipes. You'll find an inventive and concise array of seafood, pasta and meat dishes, with the option of selecting your own tasting menus. Ingredients are seasonal and local (the suppliers are listed on the menu) and the wines

Borgo Antico

come from small vineyards, as you might expect from a restaurant that is underpinned by personal values. €€€

La Casalinga

MAP PAGE 94, POCKET MAP C7
Via del Michelozzo 9r.
🌐 trattorialacasalinga.it.

Located in a side street off Piazza di Santo Spirito, this long-established family-run trattoria serves up some of the best low-cost Tuscan dishes in town. No frills – paper tablecloths, house wine by the flask and brisk service – but most nights it's filled with regulars and some tourists, and if you turn up after 8pm without a reservation you'll almost certainly have to queue. €

La Vecchia Maniera

MAP PAGE 94–107, POCKET MAP B6
Borgo San Frediano 49r. ☎ 055 264 5499.

A small and homely trattoria, serving classic Tuscan peasant fare (tripe, wild boar, mixed grills) at low prices. Unlike many Oltrarno restaurants, its clientele is predominantly local, so far. €

Osteria Antica Mescita San Niccolò

MAP PAGE 98, POCKET MAP F8
Via San Niccolò 60r. 🌐 osteriasanniccolo.it.

This genuine old-style *osteria* has a small menu of robust and well-prepared Florentine staples (*ribollita*, *lampredotto*, etc). The downstairs dining room is an atmospheric spot – it was formerly a crypt of the adjacent church of San Niccolò. €

Osteria Santo Spirito

MAP PAGE 94, POCKET MAP C7
Piazza di Santo Spirito 16r.
🌐 facebook.com/osteriasantospiritofirenze.

Run by the owners of the *Borgo Antico* (see page 107), this modern *osteria* is likewise a place that aims to please the tourists, yet does so without sacrificing its integrity. The menu is full of the usual Tuscan meat and fish dishes, but with a

Quattro Leoni

touch of contemporary flair – and the portions are substantial. Tables are on two floors, and in summer you can eat outdoors on the piazza. €€

Quattro Leoni

MAP PAGE 94, POCKET MAP C7
Via dei Vellutini 1r/Piazza della Passera.
ⓦ **4leoni.com.**
One of the most pleasant places to eat in Florence: inside, there are three rooms with splashy modern paintings hung on the rough stone walls; outside, the tables are shaded by vast canvas umbrellas in a corner of the tiny Piazza della Passera. Some say the quality of the food and service has declined with its rising popularity, but it's generally a cut above the average. €

Sabatino

MAP PAGE 94, POCKET MAP A5
Via Pisani 2r. ⓦ **trattoriasabatino.it.**
The cooking at *Sabatino* is as plain as can be, as is the place itself –

there's one refectory-like dining room, with big tables covered with laminated chequered cloth. But this old-fashioned family *osteria* is absolutely authentic, and it's ridiculously inexpensive. Italian cities used to have plenty of family-run no-nonsense *osterie* like this; in Florence, *Sabatino* is now one of a kind. €

Classical music & dance

Teatro Goldoni

MAP PAGE 94, POCKET MAP B8
Via Santa Maria 15. ⓦ **goldoniteatro.it.**
This exquisite little theatre, inaugurated in 1817 and seating just 363 people, is used for chamber music, opera and dance performances. Designed by architect Giuseppe Del Rosso the theatre has beautiful interiors, complementing the shows on stage.

The city outskirts

Two of the attractions covered in this section – the Museo Stibbert and Florence's football ground – are a stiff walk from the centre of town, but can be reached easily by public transport; the Cascine park is a stroll west from the Ognissanti district.

The Cascine

MAP PAGE 110, POCKET MAP A4
Bus #1, 9, 12, 17 or 17c from the station, or tram.

Florence's **public park**, the **Cascine**, begins close to the Ponte della Vittoria, a half-hour walk west of the Ponte Vecchio, and dwindles away 3km downstream, at the confluence of the Arno and the Mugnone rivers. Once a dairy farm (*cascina*), then a hunting reserve, this narrow strip of greenery mutated into a high-society venue in the eighteenth century: Florence's *beau monde* used to relax with a promenade under the trees of the Cascine. A fountain in the park bears a dedication to Shelley, who was inspired to write his *Ode to the West Wind* while strolling here on a blustery day in 1819.

Thousands of people come out here on Tuesday mornings for the colossal **market**, and on any day of the week the Cascine swarms with joggers, cyclists and roller-bladers. Parts of the park have become markedly gentrified of late, with the closure of the huge clubs that for years were a fixture of Florence's nightlife scene, and the opening in 2014 of the Opera di Firenze concert hall at the entrance, next to the Stazione Leopolda exhibition space.

The Museo Stibbert

MAP PAGE 110, POCKET MAP E1
Via Stibbert 26. Ⓦ museostibbert.it. Charge.

About 1500m north of San Marco stands the **Museo Stibbert**. This rambling, murky mansion was the home of the half-Scottish,

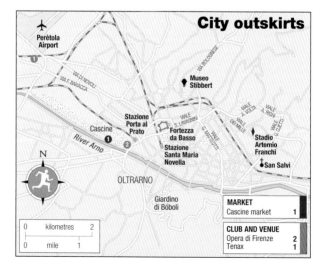

City outskirts

MARKET	
Cascine market	1

CLUB AND VENUE	
Opera di Firenze	2
Tenax	1

The Museo Stibbert

half-Italian Frederick Stibbert, who in his twenties made a name for himself in Garibaldi's army. Later he inherited a fourteenth-century house from his mother, then bought the neighbouring mansion and joined the two together, thus creating a place big enough to accommodate the fruits of his compulsive collecting. The 64 rooms contain over fifty thousand items, ranging from snuffboxes to paintings by Carlo Crivelli and a possible Botticelli.

Militaria were Frederick's chief enthusiasm, and the Stibbert **armour** collection is reckoned one of the world's best. It includes Roman, Etruscan and Japanese examples (the highlight of the whole museum), as well as a fifteenth-century *condottiere*'s outfit and the armour worn by the great Medici soldier Giovanni delle Bande Nere, retrieved from his grave in San Lorenzo in 1857. The big production number comes in the great hall, between the two houses, where a platoon of mannequins is clad in full sixteenth-century gear.

Stadio Artemio Franchi

MAP PAGE 110, POCKET MAP H3
Viale Manfredo Fanti. Ⓦ acffiorentina.com.
Bus #17 or train to Campo di Marte.
As befits this monument-stuffed city, Florence's football team, ACF Fiorentina, play in a **stadium** that's listed as a building of cultural significance, the **Stadio Artemio Franchi** (or Stadio Comunale) at Campo di Marte. It was designed by Pier Luigi Nervi in 1930, and was the first major sports venue to exploit the shape-making potential of reinforced concrete – its spiral ramps, cantilevered roof and slim central tower still make quite an impact.

Following bankruptcy in 2002, Fiorentina was kicked out of Serie A and demoted to Serie C2B, the bottom of the heap. Most of its star players jumped ship, but the club fought its way back up the leagues, returning to Serie A for the 2004/2005 season.

Supporters at Stadio Artemio Franchi

ACF Fiorentina (known as The Viola, after their violet shirts) are now once again a top-flight outfit, albeit not one of the best; they came eighth in Serie A in the 2022/23 season. Tickets cost from around €20 and can be bought at the ground itself or from numerous outlets in the city, the chief of which are Box Office and the kiosk in Via Anselmi, off Piazza della Repubblica; other points of sale are listed on the club website.

San Salvi

MAP PAGE 110, POCKET MAP H5
Via San Salvi 16. Free.

Twenty minutes' walk beyond Piazza Beccaria, east of Sant'Ambrogio, is the ex-convent of **San Salvi**, where the most precious possession is a glorious *Last Supper* by Andrea del Sarto. As a prelude to this picture, there's a gallery of fairly unremarkable Renaissance art, and some beautiful reliefs from the tomb of Giovanni Gualberto, founder of the Vallombrosan order to which this monastery belonged. The tomb was smashed up by Charles V's troops in 1530, but they refused to damage the *Last Supper*, which is still in the refectory for which it was painted, accompanied by a pair of del Sarto frescoes brought here from other churches in Florence.

Fashion factory outlets

Tuscany is the powerhouse of the country's textile industry, and several retail outlets within easy reach of Florence sell each season's leftovers with discounts as high as seventy percent.

Barberino Designer Outlet Via Meucci, Barberino di Mugello. ⓦ mcarthurglen.it/barberino. This is Barberino's biggest outlet, with some 200 brands on sale, including Furla, Guess, Michael Kors and Trussardi. Busitalia from Via Santa Caterina da Siena or shuttle bus from outside Santa Maria Novella station (2 daily).

Dolce & Gabbana Via Pian dell'Isola 49, Località Santa Maria Maddalena. ⓣ 055 833 1300. This two-storey shed is packed with clothes, accessories and household items from Dolce & Gabbana. Train to Rignano sull'Arno-Reggello, then a taxi.

The Mall Via Europa 8, Leccio Regello. ⓦ themall.it. The Mall has outlets for Cavalli, Ferragamo and Bottega Veneta, among others, but Gucci dominates. Busitalia from Via Santa Caterina da Siena or shuttle bus from Santa Maria Novella station (3 daily).

Space Via Aretina 403, Montevarchi. ⓣ 055 919 6528. Stacked with Prada clothes, and a good selection from the Miu Miu diffusion label. Train to Montevarchi, then a taxi.

Market

Cascine market

MAP PAGE 110, POCKET MAP A4
The biggest of all Florence's markets takes place on Tuesday mornings between 8am and 2pm at the Cascine park, near the banks of the Arno, where hundreds of stallholders set up an alfresco budget-class department store. Clothes (some secondhand) and shoes are the best bargains.

Club & venue

Opera di Firenze

MAP PAGE 110, POCKET MAP A4
Viale Fratelli Rosselli 1.
Ⓦ maggiofiorentino.com.
The city's hi-tech concert hall is the centrepiece of the "Parco della Musica", a cultural zone that's being developed on the edge of the Cascine park. For operas and other big events there's a 1800-seat auditorium, complemented by a 1100-seater for recitals and a terrace for open-air performances on the roof. The TI tram from Santa Maria Novella stops right outside the venue.

Tenax

MAP PAGE 110, POCKET MAP A3
Via Pratese 46. Ⓦ tenax.org.
Florence's top-ranking club, the warehouse-styled *Tenax* hosts big-name DJs. As it's located northwest, near the airport (take a taxi), you'll escape the *internazionalisti* who tend to pack the central clubs. With two large floors, it's a venue for concerts as well. In summer, when the club is shut, *Tenax* often holds one-off events at the Stazione Leopoldina, the disused train station by the new opera house. Admission from around €20.

Opera di Firenze

Fiesole

The hill-town of Fiesole, which spreads over a cluster of hills above the Mugnone and Arno valleys some 8km northeast of Florence, is conventionally described as a pleasant retreat from the crowds and heat of summertime Florence. Unfortunately, its tranquillity has been so well advertised that in high season it's now hardly less busy than Florence itself; that said, Fiesole offers a grandstand view of the city, has something of the feel of a country village, and bears many traces of its long history. First settled in the Bronze Age, later by the Etruscans and then absorbed by the Romans, it rivalled its neighbour until the early twelfth century, when the Florentines overran the town. From that time, it became a satellite, favoured as a semi-rural second home for wealthier citizens such as the ubiquitous Medici. The #7 Autolinee Toscane bus runs every twenty minutes from Via La Pira (near the junction with Piazza San Marco) to Fiesole's central Piazza Mino da Fiesole; the journey takes around twenty minutes.

The Duomo

MAP PAGE 115
Free.

When the Florentines wrecked Fiesole in 1125, the only major

Teatro Romano

building they spared was the **Duomo**, on the edge of Piazza Mino. Subsequently, nineteenth-century restorers managed to ruin the exterior, which is now notable only for its lofty campanile. The most interesting part of the bare interior is the raised choir: the altarpiece is a polyptych, painted in the 1440s by Bicci di Lorenzo, and the Cappella Salutati, to the right, contains two fine pieces carved around the same time by Mino da Fiesole – an altar frontal of *The Madonna and Saints* and the tomb of Bishop Salutati. Fiesole's patron saint, St Romulus, is buried underneath the choir in the ancient crypt.

The Museo Bandini

MAP PAGE 115
Via Dupré 1. Ⓦ museidifiesole.it. Charge, joint tickets available with other sights.
The **Museo Bandini** possesses a workaday collection of glazed terracotta in the style of the

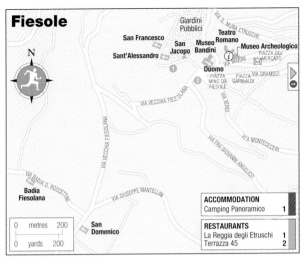

Fiesole

Giardini Pubblici
Teatro Romano
San Francesco
San Jacopo
Museo Bandini
Museo Archeologico
Sant'Alessandro
Duomo
PIAZZA
MINO DA
FIESOLE
PIAZZA
GARIBALDI
VIA GRAMSCI
PIAZZA DEL MERCATO
VIA MARINI
VIA D. MURA ETRUSCHE
N
VIA VECCHIA FIESOLANA
VIA VECCHIA FIESOLANA
VIA VERDI
VIA A. MONTECECERI
VIA FRA GIOVANNI ANGELICO
VIA BADIA D. ROCCETTINI
VIA GIUSEPPE MANTELLINI
Badia
Fiesolana
San
Domenico

| 0 | metres | 200 |
| 0 | yards | 200 |

ACCOMMODATION	
Camping Panoramico	1

RESTAURANTS	
La Reggia degli Etruschi	1
Terrazza 45	2

della Robbias, the odd piece of Byzantine ivory work and a few thirteenth- and fourteenth-century Tuscan pictures, none of them especially outstanding.

Teatro Romano and the Museo Archeologico

MAP PAGE 115
Via Portigiani 1. Ⓦ museidifiesole.it.
Charge, joint tickets available with other sights.

Built in the first century BC, the 3000-seat **Teatro Romano** was excavated towards the end of the nineteenth century and is in such good repair that it's used for performances during the Estate Fiesolana festival (see page 135). Most of the exhibits in the site's small museum were excavated in this area, and encompass pieces from the Bronze Age to the Roman occupation.

San Jacopo

MAP PAGE 115
Via San Francesco. Free.

From the piazza, the steep Via San Francesco runs past the **Oratorio di San Jacopo**, a little chapel containing a fifteenth-century fresco of *The Coronation of the*

Virgin and some fine examples of ecclesiastical goldsmithing. A little further up, on the left, a terrace in front of the town's war memorials offers a knockout view of Florence.

Sant'Alessandro

MAP PAGE 115
Via San Francesco. Free.

The church of **Sant'Alessandro**, at the top of Via San Francesco, was founded in the sixth century on the site of Etruscan and Roman temples; repairs have rendered the outside a whitewashed nonentity, but the beautiful *marmorino cipollino* (onion marble) columns of the basilical interior make it the most atmospheric building in Fiesole. The bases and Ionic capitals of the columns were recycled from Roman structures. From time to time the church is used as an exhibition space; otherwise, it's very rarely open.

San Francesco

MAP PAGE 115
Via San Francesco. Free.

The site of Fiesole's Etruscan acropolis is occupied by the fourteenth-century monastery of San Francesco. Its tranquil little church – which was rebuilt in neo-Gothic style in the first decade of the twentieth century – contains an *Immaculate Conception* by Piero di Cosimo (second altar on the right), and has a fine main altarpiece by Neri di Bicci. In the monastery's tiny **museum** you can see a miscellany of mostly unlabelled material, much of it gathered in the course of missions to the Far East; alongside the Ming and Qing vases, there's a small array of stuff from ancient Egypt. To the right of the church is a tiny and bucolic cloister, which usually can be admired only through the gate.

From the front of San Francesco a gate opens into the wooded Giardino Pubblico, the most pleasant descent back to Piazza Mino; on the way down, you'll get a good view of the Roman ruins.

San Domenico

MAP PAGE 115
Piazza San Domenico. Free.

The most enjoyable excursion from Fiesole is a wander down the narrow Via Vecchia Fiesolana, which passes the **Villa Medici** – built for Cosimo il Vecchio by Michelozzo – on its way to the hamlet of **San Domenico**. Fra' Angelico entered the Dominican order at the monastery of San Domenico, and the church retains a *Madonna and Angels* by him – it was painted for the high altar but is now in the first chapel on the left. The adjacent chapterhouse also has a Fra' Angelico fresco of *The Crucifixion* and a *Madonna and Child* that's been attributed to him; for admission, ring at no. 4, to the right of the church. The bus back to Florence stops at San Domenico, so you don't have to trudge back up to Piazza Mino to catch it.

The Badìa Fiesolana

MAP PAGE 115
Via dei Roccettini. Free.

Five minutes' walk northwest from San Domenico stands the **Badìa Fiesolana**, Fiesole's

Convento di San Francesco

Via San Francesco

cathedral from the ninth century to the beginning of the eleventh. Tradition has it that the building stands on the spot on which St Romulus was martyred during the reign of Domitian. Cosimo il Vecchio had the church altered in the 1460s, a project which left the magnificent Romanesque facade embedded in the rough stone frontage while the interior was transformed into a superb Renaissance building – the design is based on one drawn up by Brunelleschi. The monastic complex is now home to the European University Institute, an elite postgraduate research unit.

Restaurants

La Reggia degli Etruschi

MAP PAGE 115
Via San Francesco 18.
Ⓦ lareggiadeglietruschi.com.
As you'd expect, Fiesole has a few restaurants to cater for the day-trippers from Florence, but none is better than this place – the food is good, but what makes the place really memorable is the view from its dining rooms and terraces. €€

Terrazza 45

MAP PAGE 115
Piazza Mino da Fiesole 45. Ⓦ terrazza45.it.
Run by a young and very hospitable team, *Terrazza 45* is a relative newcomer to Fiesole, but it has quickly established an excellent reputation. You can eat in the stylishly monochrome dining-room or, in summer, on the panoramic terrace. Emphasis is inevitably on meat (try the *tortelli* with wild game sauce), but with a few surprises, such as fried *baccalà* (cod). €€

ACCOMMODATION

Palazzo Guadagni's lovely loggia

Accommodation

Demand for accommodation in Florence is almost limitless, which means that prices are high and some hoteliers less than scrupulous. There's rarely a let-up in the tourist invasion: "low season" is officially the period from mid-November to mid-March (except for Christmas and New Year), plus the weeks from mid-July to the end of August, when many restaurants and other outlets in the city close as Italians flee the city for the summer, but any time between March and October you should book your room well in advance. Never respond to the touts who hang around the train station: their hotels are likely to be expensive, or remote, or unlicensed private houses. Hotel prices in Florence are higher than anywhere else in Tuscany, but many places reduce their rates considerably in low season. The prices bands we've given reflect the quoted rates for one night in a standard double during high season; bear in mind that many hotels require a two-night-minimum booking at busy times.

Piazza del Duomo and around

BAVARIA MAP PAGE 28, POCKET MAP D11. Borgo degli Albizi 26. Ⓦ hotel bavariafirenze.it. A simple and friendly one-star near the city centre, occupying part of a sixteenth-century palazzo. Has just nine rooms, including several inexpensive ones with shared bathroom. Be sure to book, as it's popular with student tour groups (don't expect a quiet night). €

BENIVIENI MAP PAGE 28, POCKET MAP C11. Via delle Oche 5. Ⓦ hotelbenivieni.

it. This small, family-run three-star is situated between the Duomo and Piazza della Signoria, tucked away on a quiet backstreet. Fifteen rooms are ranged around two floors of a former synagogue; the rooms on the upper floor are brighter but all are simple, modern and in perfect condition. €

BRUNELLESCHI MAP PAGE 28, POCKET MAP C11. Piazza Santa Elisabetta 3. Ⓦ brunelleschihotelflorence.com. Designed by architect Italo Gamberini, this four-star hotel is built around a Byzantine chapel and fifth-century tower – the city's oldest building. A small in-house

Accommodation price codes

Throughout the Guide, accommodation is categorized according to a code, which roughly corresponds to the following price ranges. Price categories reflect the cost of a double room, without breakfast, in peak season.
€ = up to €200
€€ = €200–400
€€€ = over €400

Our top hotels and residenze

For a damn-the-cost weekend: *Helvetia & Bristol* see page 121
For a romantic break: *Morandi alla Crocetta* see page 124
For a room with a view: *La Scaletta* see page 125
For luxury on a budget: *Antica Dimora Firenze* see page 123
For a touch of history: *Brunelleschi* see page 120 or *Antica Torre di Via Tornabuoni* see page 122
The best in Oltrarno: *Palazzo Guadagni* see page 125
If you're really watching the pennies: *Cestelli* see page 122

museum displays Roman and other fragments found during building work. Décor is simple and stylishly modern, with earthen tones predominant; the 96 rooms and suites are spacious – the best, on the fourth floor, have views of the Duomo and Campanile. €€€

HELVETIA & BRISTOL MAP PAGE 28, POCKET MAP B11. Via dei Pescioni 2. Ⓦ hotelhelvetiabristol.com. In business since 1894 and favoured by such luminaries as Pirandello, Stravinsky and Gary Cooper, this is undoubtedly Florence's finest small five-star hotel. The public spaces and 67 bedrooms and suites (each unique) are faultlessly designed and fitted, mixing antique furnishings and modern facilities – such as jacuzzis in many bathrooms – to create a style that evokes the Belle Epoque without being twee. If you're going to treat yourself, this is a leading contender. €€€

MAXIM MAP PAGE 28, POCKET MAP C11. Entrances at Via dei Calzaiuoli 11 (lift) and Via de' Medici 4 (stairs). Ⓦ hotelmaximfirenze.it. Few three-star hotels offer a better location than this friendly 26-room place just a minute from the Duomo. The clean double rooms are excellent value, and all have en-suite bathrooms; the quietest look onto a central courtyard. €

RESIDENZA DEI PUCCI MAP PAGE 28, POCKET MAP E4. Via dei Pucci 9. Ⓦ residenzadeipucci.com. Located very close to the Duomo, the *Residenza dei Pucci* occupies a fine nineteenth-century townhouse, and offers six beautifully furnished and airy rooms, each of them different from all the others. €

IL SALOTTO DI FIRENZE MAP PAGE 28, POCKET MAP C10. Via Roma 6. Ⓦ difirenze. eu. This *residenza* has six well-appointed rooms, with three overlooking Piazza del Duomo. Perhaps not a good choice if you're a light sleeper, but the standard of accommodation is high and the location unbeatable. €

SAVOY MAP PAGE 28, POCKET MAP C11. Piazza della Repubblica 7. Ⓦ roccofortehotels.com. Fitted out in discreetly luxurious modern style, with plenty of bare wood, stone-coloured fabrics and peat-coloured marble, the *Savoy* is one of the city's very best hotels. Some might find it a bit too business-like, but the efficiency of the operation is impressive. And the location could not be better. €€€

Piazza della Signoria and around

HERMITAGE MAP PAGE 38, POCKET MAP B13. Vicolo Marzio 1/Piazza del Pesce. Ⓦ hermitagehotel.com. Pre-booking is recommended year-round to secure one of the 28 rooms in this three-star hotel right next to the Ponte Vecchio, with unbeatable views from some rooms as well as from the flower-filled roof garden. The service is friendly, and rooms are cosy, decorated with the odd antique flourish; bathrooms are small but nicely done. €€

RELAIS CAVALCANTI MAP PAGE 38, POCKET MAP B12. Via Pellicceria 2. Ⓦ relaiscavalcanti.com. Run by Francesca and her sister Anna, the *Relais Cavalcanti* is a homely fourth-floor guesthouse that occupies the fourth floor of a palazzo overlooking the Palazzo di Parte Guelfa and

Porcellino market. The rooms are a good size and are perfectly maintained, and the location is excellent. There's a bar on the ground floor, but the glazing more than takes care of any noise. €

RESIDENZA D'EPOCA IN PIAZZA DELLA SIGNORIA MAP PAGE 38, POCKET MAP D12. Via dei Magazzini 2. ⓦ boutiquehotelinpiazza.com. This luxurious *residenza d'epoca* has ten spacious bedrooms, several of them giving a view of the piazza. The style is antique, but tastefully restrained, and the management is very friendly. €€

West of the centre

ALESSANDRA MAP PAGE 54, POCKET MAP B13. Borgo Santi Apostoli 17. ⓦ hotelalessandra.com. An unpretentious and very good two-star, with 27 rooms (nearly all with bathroom) occupying a sixteenth-century palazzo and furnished in a mixture of antique and modern styles. Not the cheapest two-star in town, but among the most comfortable. €

ANTICA TORRE DI VIA TORNABUONI MAP PAGE 54, POCKET MAP A12. Via Tornabuoni 1. ⓦ tornabuoni1.com. Based in a medieval building, a more conveniently located and characterful hotel you will not find. Right in the centre of Florence and overlooking the Arno, *Antica Torre* boasts two stunning and relaxing roof terraces from which you can sip a delicious Negroni while enjoying views over the city to challenge even those from the Duomo. Extremely pricey, but well worth it. €€€

BRETAGNA MAP PAGE 54, POCKET MAP C6. Lungarno Corsini 6. ⓦ hotelbretagna. net. This three-star riverfront hotel has a superb location and Rococo-style breakfast and living rooms. Six of the 24 rooms overlook the Arno, and most of the rest have en-suite bathrooms and a/c. €€

CESTELLI MAP PAGE 54, POCKET MAP A12. Borgo SS Apostoli 25. ⓦ hotelcestelli. com. Spotlessly maintained by its Florentine and Japanese owners, this eight-roomed one-star occupies part of a house that once belonged to a minor Medici, whose bust adorns the facade. The rooms are a good size, and most are en suite. €

DIMORA PALANCA MAP PAGE 54, POCKET MAP A3. Via della Scala 72. ⓦ dimorapalanca.com. A short walk out of the city centre affords this five-star boutique hotel an unusual level of peace and quiet. With stunningly romantic double rooms, communal areas that retain beautiful ceiling frescoes, and suites for families, the building was previously a meeting place for artists and musicians. Breakfast is particularly delicious. €€€

ELITE MAP PAGE 54, POCKET MAP C4. Via della Scala 12. ☎ 0327 329 5637. Of all the hotels on this street, the ten-room two-star *Elite* is a bargain. It's basic but clean and is run by very pleasant management. Most rooms have private bathrooms; ask for a room at the back, as Via della Scala is quite a busy road. €

GALLERY HOTEL ART MAP PAGE 54, POCKET MAP B13. Vicolo dell'Oro 5. ⓦ lungarnohotels.com. In a small, quiet

Rooms for rent

To be classified as a hotel in Florence, a building has to have at least seven bedrooms. Places with fewer rooms operate as *affitacamere* ("rooms for rent") or *residenze d'epoca* (if occupying a historic building) – though, confusingly, a *residenza d'epoca* might have as many as a dozen rooms. Some *affitacamere* are just a couple of rooms in a private house, but several – and most *residenze d'epoca* – are small hotels in all but name, offering some of the most atmospheric accommodation in Florence. Many *affitacamere* are on the upper floors of large buildings, and can be reached only by stairs.

square a few paces from the Ponte Vecchio, this immensely stylish four-star is unlike any other hotel in central Florence. Owned by the Ferragamo fashion house, it has a sleek, minimalist and hyper-modern look – lots of dark wood and neutral colours – and tasteful contemporary art displayed in the reception and all 74 rooms. There's a small but smart bar, a sushi restaurant and an attractive lounge with art-filled bookshelves and comfortable sofas. €€€

J.K. PLACE MAP PAGE 54, POCKET MAP C5. Piazza Santa Maria Novella 7. Ⓦjkplace. com. One of the most appealing of Florence's designer hotels occupies a fine eighteenth-century building on Piazza Santa Maria Novella. The twenty rooms of this elegant townhouse have been designed by Michele Bönan in retro-modernist hybrid style, and have DVD players and flat-screen TVs. €€€

NIZZA MAP PAGE 54, POCKET MAP A10. Via del Giglio 5. Ⓦhotelnizza.com. A smart eighteen-room family-run two star, with helpful staff and a very central location. All rooms are en suite, and are better furnished and decorated than many in this category. €

PALAZZO DI CAMUGLIANO MAP PAGE 54. POCKET MAP C5. Via del Moro 15. Ⓦpalazzodicamugliano.com. Occupying part of a sixteenth-century mansion between Piazza Santa Maria Novella and river, this is a palatial and tranquil *residenza*, strewn with antiques and adorned with frescoes and rich stuccowork. Most of the ten rooms have a four-poster bed and beautiful wood-beam ceilings, and some of them are immense. €€

PORTA ROSSA MAP PAGE 54, POCKET MAP A12. Via Porta Rossa 19. Ⓦbit.ly/ NHPortaRossa. Florence's most venerable five-star hotel, the 72-room *Porta Rossa* has been in business since the beginning of the nineteenth century and has hosted, among others, Byron and Stendhal. Retaining something of its old ambience, the rooms have been fitted out in crisp but luxuriously modern style, with red and white the dominant tones. €€

TORRE GUELFA MAP PAGE 54, POCKET MAP B12. Borgo SS Apostoli 8.

Ⓦhoteltorreguelfa.com. Twenty tastefully furnished rooms are crammed into the third floor of this ancient tower, the tallest private building in the city; there are marvellous views from the small roof garden. There are also six cheaper doubles on the first floor (no TV and more noise from the road). Though slightly shabby in places, this is a characterful hotel, and very popular. €€

North of the centre

ANTICA DIMORA FIRENZE MAP PAGE 68, POCKET MAP F2. Via San Gallo 72. Ⓦantichedimorefiorentine.it. This plush *residenza*, run by the owners of the neighbouring *Antica Dimora Johlea* (see below), has six very comfortable double rooms, some with four-poster beds. €

ANTICA DIMORA JOHLEA MAP PAGE 68, POCKET MAP F2. Via San Gallo 80. Ⓦantichedimorefiorentine.it. Slightly pricier and a little more luxurious than the *Antica Dimora Firenze*, this lovely *residenza* also has a nice roof terrace, giving a roofline view of the Duomo and the hills beyond. €

AZZI MAP PAGE 68, POCKET MAP D4. Via Faenza 56. Ⓦhotelazzi.com. This immensely welcoming three-star has fifteen bedrooms decorated in a cozily rustic style, with antique furnishings and garden views from most rooms. The owners are keen musicians, and sometimes put on a song recital for guests, with *aperitivi*. €

CASCI MAP PAGE 68, POCKET MAP E4. Via Cavour 13. ☎055 211 686. It would be hard to find a more hospitable two-star in central Florence than this 26-room family-run hotel, which occupies part of a building in which Rossini once stayed. Only two (sound-proofed) rooms face the busy street; the rest are very quiet, and all are clean and neat, if somewhat compact. The welcome is unfailingly warm, the owners are immensely helpful, and the buffet breakfast – laid out under the frescoed ceiling of the reception area – is generous. €

KURSAAL & AUSONIA MAP PAGE 68, POCKET MAP D3. Via Nazionale 24.

Ⓦ kursonia.com. Welcoming, recently refurbished three-star near the station, with accommodation ranging from spacious "superior" doubles, in faux-antique style, to rather more bland and functional "standard" rooms. €

LOCANDA DEI POETI MAP PAGE 68, POCKET MAP D3. Via Guelfa 74.

Ⓦ locandadeipoeti.com. Run by an actor and his partner, this small B&B has a poetry theme, as you might have guessed. Various parts of the building are dedicated to different poets, and poems are written on some of the walls. The wackiness doesn't extend to the four individually styled bedrooms, however. €

LOGGIATO DEI SERVITI MAP PAGE 68, POCKET MAP F3. Piazza Santissima Annunziata 3. Ⓦ loggiatodeiservitihotel.

it. Elegant three-star in one of Florence's most celebrated squares. Its 38 rooms have been incorporated into a structure designed in the sixteenth century in imitation of the Brunelleschi hospital across the square, to accommodate the Servite priests who worked there. The plainness of some rooms reflects something of the building's history, but all are decorated with fine fabrics and antiques, and look out either onto the piazza or peaceful gardens to the rear: top-floor rooms have glimpses of the Duomo. The five rooms in the nearby annexe, at Via dei Servi 49, are similarly styled, but the building doesn't have the same charisma. €€

MERLINI MAP PAGE 68, POCKET MAP D3. Via Faenza 56. Ⓦ hotelmerlini.it.

Several budget hotels are crammed into this address, and the family-run *Merlini*, on the third floor (no lift), is one of the best. Its ten rooms have marble bathrooms – an unexpected bonus in this price bracket – and six give views of the Duomo. €

MORANDI ALLA CROCETTA MAP PAGE 68, POCKET MAP G3. Via Laura 50.

Ⓦ hotelmorandi.it. An intimate three-star gem, whose small size and friendly welcome ensure a home-from-home atmosphere. Rooms are tastefully decorated with antiques and old prints, and vivid carpets laid on parquet floors. Two rooms

have balconies opening onto a modest garden; another – with fresco fragments and medieval nooks and crannies – was converted from the site's former convent chapel. €

MR. MY RESORT MAP PAGE 68, POCKET MAP E2. Via delle Ruote 14a.

Ⓦ mrflorence.it. Run by the same friendly family as *Relais Grand Tour* (see below), this luxury B&B has five bright, quirkily furnished rooms arranged around a tranquil garden, but the real draw is the private, stone-walled spa in the basement, complete with Turkish bath and jacuzzi. €

ORTO DE' MEDICI MAP PAGE 68, POCKET MAP E3. Via San Gallo 30. Ⓦ ortodeimedici.

it. A 31-room frescoed and antique-furnished three-star, occupying a quiet palazzo in the university area. Via San Gallo is not the most attractive street in Florence, but the hotel has a nice formal garden and has been very impressively refurbished; its off-season rates are terrific too. €€

RELAIS GRAND TOUR MAP PAGE 68, POCKET MAP E3. Via Santa Reparata 21. Ⓦ florencegrandtour.com. The very hospitable owners have done a great job in turning two floors of this old palazzo, adjoining an eighteenth-century private theatre, into a superb guesthouse, with three large bedrooms upstairs and three suites on the ground floor. Each room is unique – one suite has Neapolitan majolica tiles in the bathroom, while another (formerly a dressing-room) is loaded with antique mirrors. €

RESIDENZA CASTIGLIONI MAP PAGE 68, POCKET MAP D4. Via del Giglio 8.

Ⓦ residenzacastiglioni.com. This discreet and hugely stylish hideaway has just half a dozen spacious en-suite double rooms (three of them frescoed), on the second floor of a palazzo very close to San Lorenzo church. Room 22 is one to go for, with wall-to-wall frescoes. €€

RESIDENZA JOHANNA I MAP PAGE 68, POCKET MAP E2. Via Bonifacio Lupi 14.

Ⓦ antichedimorefiorentine.it. The longest-established of the *Johanna/Johlea* family of *residenze*, this genteel place is hidden away in an unmarked apartment building in a quiet, leafy corner of the city, a 5min walk north of San Marco. Rooms are cosy and well kept, and the management are as friendly and helpful as you could hope for. €

East of the centre

DALÌ MAP PAGE 84, POCKET MAP F5. Via dell' Oriuolo 17. Ⓦ hoteldali.com. One of the least expensive one-star options close to the centre, with just nine rooms, five with bath. The rooms are plain and rather basic, but the location – on the top floor of a palazzo built in 1492 – helps, as does the view from the back rooms of the giant magnolia in the garden below. The friendly owners speak good English. €

J & J MAP PAGE 84, POCKET MAP G5. Via di Mezzo 20. ☎ 055 263 12. The bland exterior of this former fifteenth-century convent conceals a romantic nineteen-room four-star hotel. Some rooms are vast split-level affairs, but all have charm and are furnished with modern fittings and a few antiques. Common areas are decked with flowers, and retain frescoes and vaulted ceilings from the original building. In summer, breakfast is served in the convent's lovely old cloister. €€

RELAIS SANTA CROCE MAP PAGE 84, POCKET MAP F6. Via Ghibellina 87. Ⓦ florence.baglionihotels.com. This magnificent five-star shares a lobby with the mind-blowingly expensive *Pinchiorri* restaurant (see page 90), and is a similarly top-flight establishment. The grandiose public rooms are a very slick amalgam of the historic and the contemporary, with modern sofas set on acres of gleaming parquet, surrounded by eighteenth-century stucco panels. Contemporary and understated luxury prevails in the bedrooms, which are graded "superior", "deluxe" and "exclusive" (these have their own saunas). Then there are suites, which are in the "if you have to ask the price you can't afford it" category. €€€

Oltrarno

AD ASTRA MAP PAGE 94. POCKET MAP B7. Via del Campuccio 53.

Ⓦ adastraflorence.it. The spectacular *Ad Astra* is more a super-deluxe B&B than a hotel, consisting of just nine luxurious rooms, seven of which are on the ground floor of the ancestral home of the Torrigiani family (the Marchese is still in residence), with two more in an annexe in the garden, which is said to be the largest private garden in Europe. Some of the rooms open onto the huge terrace that wraps around the building, and each has been individually designed. There are plenty of antiques around the place, as you'd expect, but many of the bedroom furnishings are the work of post-war Italian designers. €€

ANNALENA MAP PAGE 94, POCKET MAP B8. Via Romana 34. ☎ 055 222 402. A short way beyond Palazzo Pitti (and right by an entrance to the Giardino di Boboli), this bargain twenty-room three-star occupies part of a building once owned by the Medici. The best rooms open onto a gallery with garden views, and a sprinkling of antiques lends a hint of old-world charm. €

PALAZZO GUADAGNI MAP PAGE 94, POCKET MAP C7. Piazza Santo Spirito 9. Ⓦ palazzoguadagni.com. This very attractive three-star hotel has 15 rooms on three floors, furnished with family antiques. The middle floor is nicest, particularly room 10, with its frescoed ceiling. The lovely loggia gets the evening sun – the perfect place to wind down with an *aperitivo*. €

LA SCALETTA MAP PAGE 94, POCKET MAP D7. Via Guicciardini 13. Ⓦ lascaletta. com. Some of the rooms in this tidy and recently refurbished sixteen-room three-star give views across to the Bóboli gardens; those on the Via Guicciardini side are double-glazed against the traffic. Drinks are served on the rooftop terraces, where you look across the Bóboli in one direction and the city in the other. All rooms are en suite and nicely decorated in creamy tones. €

TORRE DI BELLOSGUARDO MAP PAGE 94. POCKET MAP A8. Via Roti Michelozzi 2. Ⓦ torrebellosguardo.com. It's not central – it's perched on a hill about 2km from the heart of Oltrarno – but the four-star Bellosguardo is one of the most beautiful hotels in the city. Dating back to the thirteenth century and once home to Galileo, it's girdled by magnificent gardens (with a pool). Each of its 16 rooms (all uniquely and exquisitely furnished) is palatial. €€

Hostels

ACADEMY HOSTEL MAP PAGE 28, POCKET MAP E4. Via Ricasoli 9. Ⓦ academy-hostel.florence-hotels-it. com. Since opening in 2008, this modern hostel has won awards for its service and excellent facilities: set in a seventeenth-century palazzo, it offers airy, high-ceilinged rooms (from singles to six beds) and a common area with huge flat-screen TV, book and DVD library and lots of computer terminals, plus a sunny terrace. All this, and an unbeatable location – just steps from the Duomo. €

ARCHI ROSSI MAP PAGE 68, POCKET MAP D3. Via Faenza 94r. Ⓦ hostelarchirossi.com. A 5min walk from the train station, this privately-owned hostel is spotlessly clean and decorated with guests' wall-paintings and graffiti. It's popular – the 140 beds fill up quickly – and has a pleasant garden and terrace. There are some basic en-suite doubles too (on the third floor; no lift), and a restaurant serving cheap meals. Breakfast is included. Dorms/doubles €

SANTA MONACA MAP PAGE 94, POCKET MAP B6. Via Santa Monaca 6. Ⓦ ostellosantamonaca.com. This privately-owned hostel in Oltrarno has 112 beds, arranged in a dozen dorms (female-only and mixed) with between two and twenty beds. Kitchen facilities, laundry and free internet; meals are available but are not included. Curfew 2am. It's a 10min walk from the station, or take bus #11, #36 or #37 to the second stop after the bridge. €

Renting an apartment

The high cost of hotel rooms in Florence makes **self-catering** an attractive option – for the price of a week in a cramped double room in a three-star hotel you could book yourself a two-bedroom apartment right in the centre of the city. Many package-holiday companies have a few apartments in their brochures, but a trawl of the internet will throw up dozens of places at more reasonable prices. One of the best places to look is Ⓦ vrbo.com, a site which puts you in touch directly with the owners and features dozens of properties in Florence. Of course, the short-term rental market has been transformed in recent years by the meteoric rise of Ⓦ Airbnb.com. In Florence there are now more than one thousand properties that are registered on this website, offering accommodation at prices that are often lower than even the most basic B&B. However, as in many cities, Airbnb is not regarded as an entirely good thing in Florence. Owners of small hotels and B&Bs are unhappy at being undercut by private individuals who are not subject to the regulations by which official providers of accommodation have to abide, and there's general unease about the effect that the ever-increasing number of holiday rentals is having on accommodation costs for the people of Florence; in recent years, students have been protesting a lack of affordable housing in the city by camping out in tents on campus. In 2023, Florence announced a ban on new short-term private holiday rentals in this centre, which includes most Airbnbs.

Camping

CAMPING PANORAMICO MAP PAGE 125,
POCKET MAP H1. Via Peramondo 1, Fiesole.
Ⓦ **campingpanoramicofiesole.com**. Located
in Fiesole, this 120-pitch three-star site
caters for tents and campervans. It has a
bar, restaurant, pool and small supermarket;
there are also electric hook-ups, showers,
toilets, disabled toilets, washing machines
and dryers. You are welcome to borrow their
iron and store food in their fridge, as well
as making use of their free shuttle between
Florence and Fiesole. €

ESSENTIALS

Scooter crossing Ponte Santa Trìnita

Arrival

Your point of arrival is most likely to be Santa Maria Novella train station, which is located within a few minutes' walk of the heart of the historic centre: rail and bus connections from the three airports that serve the city all terminate at the station, as do international trains and buses from all over Italy.

Pisa airport

Most flights to Tuscany use Pisa's **Galileo Galilei** airport (ⓦ pisa-airport.com), 95km west of Florence and 3km from the centre of Pisa. The automated Pisa Mover rail shuttle, connecting the airport to Pisa Centrale station (every 5–8min; daily 6am–12am) takes little more than 5 minutes. Alternatively, you can take the cheaper but rather less frequent and somewhat slower VaiBus city bus to Pisa Centrale; it leaves from in front of the Arrivals hall.

The last train from Pisa Centrale to Florence is at 10.30pm, with services resuming at around 4.15am; the journey takes 60–80min. The bus company currently running connections between Pisa airport and Florence is called Sky Bus Lines Caronna; buses go regularly and take 60min if traffic is light, although at busy times it can take more than 90min. The ticket office and bus stand is to the right as you come out of Arrivals.

Perètola airport

A few airlines use Florence's small Perètola (Amerigo Vespucci) airport (ⓦ aeroporto.firenze.it), 5km northwest of the city centre. There is a half-hourly shuttle bus to the city centre called Volainbus from immediately outside the arrivals area. Tickets can be bought on board or from machines at the airport, and the journey takes about thirty minutes. Alternatively, you can take a tram to Santa Maria Novella.

Bologna airport

A few airlines use Bologna (ⓦ bologna-airport.it) as a *gateway* airport for Florence. The Marconi Express monorail opened in 2020 and departs every seven minutes or so from 5.40am until midnight every day of the year. The journey takes about seven minutes and will take you directly to Bologna's main train station, from where regular trains run to Florence's Santa Maria Novella station in about forty minutes.

The train station

Florence's central station, Santa Maria Novella ("Firenze SMN" on timetables), is located just north of the church and square of Santa Maria Novella, a few blocks west of the Duomo. In the station are an accommodation service, left-luggage facilities and a 24-hour pharmacy. While in and around the station, you should keep a close eye on your bags and valuables at all times: it's a prime hunting-ground for thieves and pickpockets. Also avoid the concourse's various taxi and hotel touts, however friendly they may appear.

Getting around

Within the historic centre, walking is generally the most efficient way of getting around, and nowadays walking is a lot more pleasant than it used to be, with the extension of the **zona a traffico limitato** (ZTL) – which limits traffic in the centre to residents' cars, delivery vehicles and public transport – to cover most of the city centre from the river to a few blocks north of the Duomo.

Buses

If you want to cross town in a hurry or visit some of the peripheral sights,

The Tramvia

The T1, the first line of the city's beleaguered Tramvia tram system, connects Scandicci, to the southwest of the city centre, with Careggi hospital in the north, via Santa Maria Novella; it's essentially a commuter line, of almost no use to tourists. In 2019 the T2 from Piazza della Libertà to Perètola airport, also via Santa Maria Novella, was finally completed; there are plans to extend the T2 past the Duomo and up to San Marco, but there is very strong resistance in the city to the idea of running a tramline past the cathedral, so the feasibility of a tunnel is now under discussion, as is another line to serve the east of the city.

your best option is to use one of the frequent and speedy **Autolinee Toscane** buses (ⓦ at-bus.it). The buses are orange, with newer models in blue as well as purple and white. You can buy a single ticket which must be used within 90min, or a multiple journey ticket which are valid for up to four journeys within a period of 90min. Buy tickets before you get on the bus; it is theoretically possible to buy them from the driver, but in practice they often don't have any (or at least, they say they don't) and won't let you on. Once you're on board, you must validate your ticket right away – there's a hefty on-the-spot fine for any passenger without a validated ticket.

Generally speaking, the front and back doors are for getting on, and the middle doors are for getting off. You can buy tickets on the Tabnet App, as well as from official ticket offices (including the official bus ticket booth in the station), machines and retailers – keep your eyes peeled for the blue Autolinee Toscane sticker. Because Autolinee Toscane runs bus services throughout Tuscany, tickets you buy in Florence are also valid for buses in Lucca, Pisa, Siena, and Arezzo, among others.

Taxis

You can't flag down a taxi in the street – you have to phone for one (ⓣ 055 4242, ⓣ 055 4798 or ⓣ 055 4390) or go to a taxi rank; key locations include the train station, Piazza della Repubblica, Piazza del Duomo, Piazza Santa Maria Novella, Piazza San Marco, Piazza Santa Croce and Piazza Santa Trìnita. If you order a cab by phone, you'll be given the car's code name – usually a town, city or country – and its number, both of which are emblazoned on the vehicle. Alternatively, you can book a taxi using an app; IT Taxi, SIXT and appTaxi are all good bets. All rides are metered; supplements are payable for journeys outside the city limits (to Fiesole, for example), and for each piece of luggage placed in the boot.

Directory A–Z

Accessible travel

As part of the European Turismo per Tutti (Tourism for All) project, Italian museum, transport and accommodation facilities for those with accessibility needs have improved remarkably in last decade or so.

However, stairs, steps and cobbles continue to present the most obvious difficulties in Florence, while other problems can arise from cars being parked thoughtlessly on narrow streets. Public transport is becoming more attuned to the needs of travellers

Florentine addresses

Note that there is a **double address system** in Florence, one for businesses and another for all other properties – that, at least, is the theory, though in fact the distinction is far from rigorous. Business addresses are followed by the letter r (for *rosso*) and are marked on the building with a red number on a white plate, sometimes with an r after the numeral, but not always. The two series are independent of each other, which means that no. 20, for example, may be a long way from no. 20r.

with disabilities, but bus services are still more of a challenge than trains. Some museums and galleries offer free tickets to visitors with disabilities or access needs, and the Uffizi is particularly forthcoming when it comes to providing accessibility information; it's always worth checking online before your visit. Another thing to bear in mind is that budget hotels often occupy the upper floors of townhouses and may not have lifts; always check before booking. John Sage's website (⊛ sagetraveling. com) is a good source of practical information.

Banks
Florence's main bank branches are around Piazza della Repubblica, but exchange booths (*cambio*) and ATM cash-card machines (*bancomat*) for Visa and MasterCard advances can be found across the city. Banks generally open Mon–Fri 8.30am–3.30pm.

Consulates
The UK consulate for northern Italy is at Via San Paolo 7, Milan ☎ 02 723 001; the US has a consulate in Florence, at Lungarno Amerigo Vespucci 38 ☎ 055 266 951.

Electricity
The supply in Italy is 220V, but anything requiring 240V will work. Most plugs have two round pins, so UK equipment will need an adapter. US equipment may require a transformer as well.

Emergencies
Police ☎ 113, or ☎ 112 for the Carabinieri (military police); fire ☎ 115; ambulance ☎ 118. If your passport is lost or stolen, go to the police (see page 134) and report it to your consulate.

Health
The Medical Service is a private service used to dealing with foreigners; they have doctors on call 24hr a day on ☎ 055 475 411 (⊛ medicalservice. firenze.it), or you can visit their clinic at Via Roma 4. Note that you'll need insurance cover to recoup the cost of a consultation. Florence's central hospital is on Piazza Santa Maria Nuova.

Left luggage
The left luggage office is at Santa Maria Novella station, by platform 16.

LGBTQ+ travellers
Attitudes to LGBTQ+ people in Florence are generally tolerant; Florence has a thriving gay scene; try Piccolo Café (⊛ instagram.com/piccolo_94) or Queer (⊛ facebook.com/queerfirenze) for starters on a queer night out, or Crisco Club (⊛ instagram.com/ crisco_club_official) is a cruising club for men. However, for the time being, Italy remains a generally conservative, Catholic country, so be aware that public displays of affection that extend much beyond hand-holding might get some sideways looks. Italy's national LGBTQ+ organization, ARCI-

Gay (ⓦarcigay.it), has a branch in Florence and is active on Instagram at ⓦinstagram.com/arcigay_firenze.

Lost property

Lost property handed in at the city or railway police ends up at Via Francesco Veracini 5 (☎055 334 802; bus #17, #29, #30 or #35).

Museum admission

All of Florence's state-run museums belong to an association called Firenze Musei (ⓦfirenzemusei.it), which sets aside a daily quota of tickets that can be reserved in advance. The Uffizi, the Accademia and the Bargello belong to this group, as do the Palazzo Pitti museums, the Bóboli gardens, the Medici chapels in San Lorenzo, the archeological museum and the San Marco museum.

You can **reserve tickets** online at ⓦfirenzemusei.it and ⓦuffizi.it, at the Firenze Musei booth at Orsanmichele, at the My Accademia bookshop at Via Ricasoli 105r and at the museums themselves (in the case of the Uffizi and Pitti). Generally, the Orsanmichele booth – which is set into the wall of

the church on the Via Calzaiuoli side – is the easiest option. Pre-booking is strongly recommended in summer for the Uffizi and the Accademia, whose allocation of reservable tickets is often sold out many days ahead.

Note that on-the-door admission to all state-run museums is free on the first Sunday of the month and for under 18s of any nationality on presenting a passport, while 18–25s from the EU get a discount with proof of identity. Nearly all of Florence's major museums are routinely **closed on Monday**, though some are open for a couple of Mondays each month. In the majority of cases, museum ticket offices close thirty minutes before the museum itself. At the Palazzo Vecchio and Museo Stibbert, however, it's one hour before, while at the Uffizi, Bargello, Museo dell'Opera del Duomo, the dome of the Duomo, the Campanile and Pitti museums it's 45 minutes.

For Florence's civic museums – of which the main ones are the Museo Bardini, Museo Santa Maria Novella, Palazzo Vecchio and the Cappella Brancacci – details can be found at ⓦmusefirenze.it.

Firenze Card

The Firenze Card, costing €85, is valid for 72 hours from the first time you use it, and gives access to 72 museums and monuments in greater Florence (including all the big ones). The card enables you to bypass the queues at the major museums, which have separate gates for card holders. You do, though, have to pack a lot into each day to make it worthwhile – for most people the 72 hours would be better spent getting the most out of a few sights, rather than racing around the city trying to justify the investment. What's more, some of the museums, such as Medici villa at Cerreto Guidi, are some distance out of the city, and are highly unlikely to feature on anyone's three-day blitz. The card can be bought at the Via Cavour and Piazza Stazione tourist offices, and at the Uffizi (door 2), Palazzo Vecchio, Bargello, Palazzo Pitti, Palazzo Strozzi, Museo Bardini and Cappella Brancacci. If bought online (ⓦfirenzecard.it), it can be collected at any of the tourist offices, Museo Bardini, Cappella Brancacci, Palazzo Vecchio or Palazzo Strozzi.

Eating out price codes

Throughout the Guide, eating out listings are categorized according to a price code, which roughly corresponds to the following price ranges. Price categories reflect the cost of a two-course meal for one, without alcohol.

€ = under €30
€€ = €30–€60
€€€ = over €60

Pharmacies

The Farmacia Comunale, at the train station, is open 24hr. All'Insegna del Moro, at Piazza San Giovanni 20r, on the north side of the Baptistery, is open from 8am to midnight every day of the year. All pharmacies display a late-night roster in their window.

Police

Emergency ☎ 112 or 113. To report a theft or other crime, go to the Carabinieri at Borgo Ognissanti 48, to the Questura at Via Zara 2, or to the tourist police at Via Pietrapiana 50r – you're more likely to find an English-speaker at the last one. If you do report a theft or other crime, you will have to fill out a form (*una denuncia*); this may be time-consuming, but it's essential if you want to make a claim on your travel insurance upon returning home.

Post office

The main central post office is near Piazza della Repubblica at Via Pellicceria 3. If all you want are stamps (*francobolli*), then it's easier to buy them at one of the city's innumerable *tabacchi*, which are marked by a sign outside with a white "T" on a blue background.

Phones

Many foreign mobile phones will automatically connect to a local provider. However, some American cellphones do not work with the Italian mobile network. Make sure you know what your providers charges for calls and data are in advance, and to check the compatibility of your phone.

Nearly all of Florence's public phones accept coins, but you get more time for your euros if you use a phone card, which can be bought from any *tabaccheria* and any shop displaying the Telecom Italia sticker.

Price codes

Accommodation (see box, page 120) and eating out listings (see box) throughout the Guide have been categorized according to a code, which correspond to price ranges.

Time

Italy is on Central European Time (CET), one hour ahead of the UK, six hours ahead of Eastern Standard Time and nine hours ahead of Pacific Standard Time.

Tourist information

The biggest and most helpful tourist office is at Via Cavour 1r, a 5min walk north of the Duomo (Mon–Sat 9am–7pm, Sun until 2pm; ☎ 055 290 832, ⓦ feelflorence.it); this office provides information not just on the city but on the whole of Florence province. There are various other infopoints around the city, including at Piazza della Stazione 4, at Perètola airport and in Fiesole.

Another excellent source of information is *Firenze Spettacolo* (ⓦ firenzespettacolo.it), a monthly, mostly bilingual listings magazine available from bookshops and larger newsstands. Also useful is *The Florentine* (⊕ theflorentine.net), a free bi-weekly English-language paper,

available at the tourist office, most bookshops and various other spots (the website lists all of the places it can be picked up).

Festivals and events

Scoppio del Carro

Easter Sunday
For Easter Sunday's Scoppio del Carro (Explosion of the Cart), a cartload of fireworks is hauled by six white oxen from the Porta a Prato to the Duomo; there, during the midday Mass, the whole lot is set off by a "dove" that whizzes down a wire from the high altar.

Festa del Grillo

First Sunday after Ascension
On the first Sunday after Ascension Day (forty days after Easter), the Festa del Grillo (Festival of the Cricket) is held in the Cascine park. In among the market stalls and the picnickers, people sell tiny mechanical crickets. Live crickets were sold until recently, a vestige of a ritual that may hark back to the days when farmers had to scour their land for locusts.

Maggio Musicale Fiorentino

May–June
⊕ maggiofiorentino.com
Confusingly, the Maggio Musicale isn't restricted to May (Maggio), but lasts for a couple of months from late April or early May. The festival has its own

orchestra, chorus and ballet company, plus guest appearances from foreign ensembles. Events are staged at the Teatro Comunale (or its Teatro Piccolo), the Teatro della Pergola, the Palazzo dei Congressi, the Teatro Verdi, the Opera di Firenze and occasionally in the Bóboli gardens. Information and tickets can be obtained from the Teatro Comunale, Corso Italia 16.

Estate Fiesolana

July–August
Much smaller and less exclusive than the Maggio Musicale, concentrating more on chamber and symphonic music, the Estate Fiesolana is held in Fiesole every summer, usually from July to late August. Films and theatre are also featured, and most events are held in the Teatro Romano.

St John's Day and the Calcio Storico

June 24 and two later dates
The saint's day of John the Baptist, Florence's patron, is June 24 – the occasion for a massive fireworks display up on Piazzale Michelangelo, and for the Calcio Storico. Played in sixteenth-century costume, this

Florence online

Agenzia per il Turismo di Firenze ⊕ feelflorence.it. The official tourist office site, with an English-language option. Useful for information on forthcoming exhibitions and hotel listings.
Firenze Spettacolo ⊕ firenzespettacolo.it. The online edition of Florence's listings magazine.
Musei Civici ⊕ musefirenze.it. Information on Florence's civic museums.

National holidays

Everything, except some bars and restaurants, closes on Italy's official **national holidays**, which are: January 1, January 6 (Epiphany), Easter Monday, April 25 (Liberation Day), May 1 (Labour Day), June 2 (Day of the Republic), August 15 (Ferragosto; Assumption), November 1 (Ognissanti; All Saints), December 8 (Immaculate Conception), December 25 and December 26.

uniquely Florentine mayhem is a three-match series culminating with the final on June 24, in Piazza Santa Croce. Each of the four historic quarters fields a team of 27 players, Santa Croce playing in blue, San Giovanni in green, Santa Maria Novella in red and Santo Spirito in impractical white. The prize for the winning side is a vast quantity of steak, equivalent to the white calf traditionally awarded to the victors. A sort of hybrid of rugby, boxing and wrestling, the game is characterized by incomprehensible rules and an extraordinary degree of violence.

Festa delle Rificolone

September 7
The Festa delle Rificolone (Festival of the Lanterns) takes place on the Virgin's birthday, September 7, with a procession of children from Santa Croce to Piazza Santissima Annunziata, where market stalls are set out for the evening. Each child carries a coloured paper lantern with a candle inside it – a throwback to the days when people from the surrounding countryside would troop by lantern light into the city for the Feast of the Virgin.

Chronology

Eighth century BC The Etruscans are settled throughout the area known as Tuscany, with their principal settlements in Roselle, Vetulonia, Populonia, Volterra, Chiusi, Cortona, Arezzo and – most northerly of all – Fiesole.

59 BC The Roman colony of Florentia is established by Julius Caesar as a settlement for army veterans. By now the Romans have either subsumed or exterminated most Etruscan towns.

Second and third centuries AD Rapid expansion of Florentia as a river port.

Fourth century AD Christianity is spreading throughout Italy. The church of San Lorenzo and the martyr's shrine at San Miniato are both established in Florentia.

552 Florence falls to the hordes of the Gothic king Totila. Less than twenty years later the Lombards storm in, subjugating the city to the duchy whose capital was in Pavia.

End of the eighth century
Charlemagne's Franks have taken control of much of Italy, with the administration overseen by imperial margraves, based in Lucca. These proxy rulers develop into some of the most powerful figures in the Holy Roman Empire and are instrumental in spreading Christianity even further.

978 Willa, widow of the margrave Uberto, establishes the Badìa in Florence, the first monastic foundation in the centre of the city.

1027 The position of margrave passes to the Canossa family, who take the title of the Counts of Tuscia (as Tuscany was then called). The most influential figure produced by this dynasty is Matilda, daughter of the first Canossa margrave.

1115 In the year of Matilda's death she grants Florence the status of an independent city. The new commune of Florence is essentially governed by a council of one hundred men, the great majority drawn from the rising merchant class. In 1125 the city's increasing dominance of the region is confirmed when it crushes the rival city of Fiesole. Fifty years later, as the population booms with the rise of the textile industry, new walls are built around what is now one of the largest cities in Europe.

Thirteenth century Throughout Tuscany, conflict develops between the Ghibelline faction and the Guelphs – the former, broadly speaking, are pro-empire, with the Guelphs defined chiefly by their loyalty to the papacy. When Charles of Anjou conquers Naples in 1266, association with the anti-imperial French becomes another component of Guelphism, and a loose Guelph alliance soon stretches from Paris to Naples, substantially funded by the bankers of Tuscany. Florence and Lucca are generally Guelph strongholds, while Pisa, Arezzo, Prato, Pistoia and Siena tend to side with the empire.

1207 Florence's governing council is replaced by the *podestà*, an executive official who is traditionally a non-Florentine. Around this time the first *arti* (guilds) are formed to promote the interests of the traders and bankers.

1248 Florence's Ghibellines enlist the help of Emperor Frederick II to oust the Guelphs, but within two years they have been displaced by the Guelph-backed regime of the Primo Popolo, a quasi-democratic government drawn from the mercantile class.

1280 Power passes to the Secondo Popolo, a regime run by the Arti Maggiori (Great Guilds). The fulcrum of power in Florence shifts definitively towards its bankers, merchants and manufacturers.

1293 The Secondo Popolo excludes the nobility from government and invests power in the Signoria, a council drawn from the Arti Maggiori.

1348 The Black Death destroys as many as half the city's population. However, the plague is equally devastating throughout the region, and does nothing to reverse the economic and political supremacy of the city.

1406 Florence takes control of Pisa and thus gains a long-coveted seaport. Despite the survival of Sienese independence into the sixteenth century, the history of Tuscany increasingly becomes the history of Florence.

1431–1434 Cosimo de' Medici is imprisoned by the city authorities, having provoked the big families of the Signoria with his support for the members of the disenfranchised lesser guilds. In 1434, after a session of the Parlamento – a general council called in times of emergency – he is invited to return. Having secured the military support of the Sforza family of Milan, Cosimo (Cosimo il Vecchio) becomes the pre-eminent figure in the city's political life for more than three decades. Florence's reputation as the most innovative cultural centre in Europe is strengthened by his patronage of Donatello, Michelozzo and a host of other artists.

1439 Council of Florence is convened, to try to reconcile the Catholic and Eastern churches. The consequent influx of Greek scholars adds momentum to the study of classical philosophy and literature.

1478 The Pazzi family conspire with Pope Sixtus IV to murder Lorenzo il Magnifico (Cosimo's grandson, and the de facto ruler of Florence) and his brother Giuliano; the plot fails, and only increases the esteem in which Lorenzo is held.

1494 Lorenzo's son Piero is obliged to flee Florence following his surrender to the invading French army of Charles VIII. This invasion is the commencement of a bloody half-century dominated by the so-called Wars of Italy.

1498 Having in effect ruled the city in the absence of the Medici, the Dominican friar Girolamo Savonarola is executed as a heretic.

1512 Following Florence's defeat by the Spanish and papal armies, the Medici return, in the person of the vicious Giuliano, Duke of Nemours.

1527 Holy Roman Emperor Charles V's army pillages Rome. The humiliation of Pope Clement VII (a Medici) spurs the people of Florence to eject his deeply unpopular relatives.

1530 After a siege by the combined papal and imperial forces, Florence is obliged to receive Alessandro, who was proclaimed Duke of Florence, the first Medici to bear the title of ruler.

1537 Alessandro is assassinated and power passes to another Cosimo (not a direct heir but rather a descendant of Cosimo il Vecchio's brother), thanks to support from the emperor Charles V, whose daughter was married to Alessandro.

1557 Cosimo buys the territory of Siena from the Habsburgs, giving Florence control of all of Tuscany with the solitary exception of Lucca. Two years later Florentine hegemony in Tuscany is confirmed in the Treaty of Cateau-Cambrésis, the final act in the Wars of Italy.

1570 Cosimo takes the title Cosimo I, Grand Duke of Tuscany. In European terms Tuscany is a second-rank power, but it's one of the strongest states in Italy. Cosimo builds the Uffizi, extends and overhauls the Palazzo Vecchio, installs the Medici in the Palazzo Pitti, has the Ponte Santa Trìnita constructed across the Arno and commissions much of the public sculpture around the Piazza della Signoria. His descendants remain in power until 1737.

1630s The market for Florence's woollen goods collapses, and the city's banks go into a terminal slump.

1737 Under the terms of a treaty signed by Anna Maria de' Medici (the sister of Gian Gastone de' Medici, the last male Medici), Florence passes to the House of Lorraine, cousins of the Austrian Habsburgs.

1799 Napoleon dislodges the Austrians from Italy, but after his fall from power the Lorraine dynasty is brought back, remaining in residence until the last of the line, Leopold II, consents to his own deposition in 1859.

1865 Florence becomes the capital of the new Kingdom of Italy, a position it holds until 1870, when Rome takes over. The city's subsequent decline is accelerated by the economic disruption that follows World War I.

1943 After the Allied landing at Monte Cassino, Tuscany is a battlefield between the Nazis and the partisans. Substantial parts of Florence are wrecked by the retreating German army, who bomb all the bridges except the Ponte Vecchio and blow up much of the medieval city near the banks of the Arno.

Since World War II After World War II the province of Florence establishes itself as the third largest industrial centre in Italy. Textiles, metalwork, glass, ceramics, pharmaceuticals and chemical production remain major industries in the province, while in Florence itself many long-established crafts continue to thrive, notably jewellery and gold-working, the manufacture of handmade paper, perfumery and leatherwork. But tourism is the mainstay of Florence's economy, with more than fifteen million overnight stays per year pre-Covid. This figure hasn't been reached again in the years since the pandemic, but the city looks set to recover and surpass this number soon.

2015 The city becomes the capital of the newly created administrative division, Metropolitan City of Florence, with Dario Nardella of the Democratic Party as Mayor of Florence; he was elected to the position the previous year, aged just 38.

2020 Covid-19 sweeps Florence and Italy as it does the world, leading to school closures, the cancellations of festivals and events, national lockdowns, travel restrictions and alarming death tolls. In an attempt to raise spirits, opera singer Maurizio Marchini belts out Nessun dorma from his balcony in Florence; a video of his performance goes viral.

2024 While Dario Nardella is the first Mayor of Florence to have his five-year mayoral term renewed, Florence gears up to elect their first new mayor in a decade in the summer of 2024.

Italian

What follows is a brief pronunciation guide and a rundown of essential words and phrases.

Pronunciation

Italian **pronunciation** is easy, since every word is spoken exactly as it is written. The only difficulties you are likely to encounter are the few consonants that are different from English:

c before e or i is pronounced as in **ch**urch, while **ch** before the same vowels is hard, as in **c**at.
sci or **sce** are pronounced as in **sh**eet and **sh**elter respectively.
g is soft before **e** and **i**, as in **g**eranium; hard when followed by **h**, as in **g**arlic.
gn has the ni sound of our "on**i**on".

gl in Italian is softened to something like li in English, as in stal**li**on.
h is not aspirated, as in **h**onour.
Nearly all Italian words are stressed on the penultimate syllable unless an accent (´ or `) denotes otherwise, although written accents are often left out in practice. Note that the ending -ia or -ie counts as two syllables, hence *trattoria* is stressed on the i.

Words and phrases

Basic words and phrases

Good morning Buongiorno
Good afternoon/evening Buonasera
Good night Buonanotte
Goodbye Arrivederci

ITALIAN

Yes Sì

No No

Please Per favore

Thank you (very much) Grazie (molte/mille grazie)

You're welcome Prego

Alright/that's OK Va bene

How are you? Come stai/sta? (informal/formal)

I'm fine Bene

Do you speak English? Parla inglese?

I don't understand Non ho capito

I don't know Non lo so

Excuse me Mi scusi/Prego

Excuse me (in a crowd) Permesso

I'm sorry Mi dispiace

I'm English Sono inglese

...Scottish ...scozzese

...American ...americano

...Irish ...irlandese

...Welsh ...gallese

Today Oggi

Tomorrow Domani

Day after tomorrow Dopodomani

Yesterday Ieri

Now Adesso

Later Più tardi

Wait a minute! Aspetta!

In the morning Di mattina

In the afternoon Nel pomeriggio

In the evening Di sera

Here/there Qui/Là

Good/bad Buono/Cattivo

Big/small Grande/Piccolo

Cheap/expensive Economico/Caro

Hot/cold Caldo/Freddo

Near/far Vicino/Lontano

Vacant/occupied Libero/Occupato

With/without Con/Senza

More/less Più/Meno

Enough, no more Basta

Mr... Signor...

Mrs... Signora...

Miss... Signorina... (il Signor, la Signora, la Signorina when speaking about someone else)

Numbers

1 uno

2 due

3 tre

4 quattro

5 cinque

6 sei

7 sette

8 otto

9 nove

10 dieci

11 undici

12 dodici

13 tredici

14 quattordici

15 quindici

16 sedici

17 diciassette

18 diciotto

19 diciannove

20 venti

21 ventuno

22 ventidue

30 trenta

40 quaranta

50 cinquanta

60 sessanta

70 settanta

80 ottanta

90 novanta

100 cento

101 centuno

110 centodieci

200 duecento

500 cinquecento

1000 mille

5000 cinquemila

10,000 diecimila

50,000 cinquantamila

Some signs

Entrata/Uscita Entrance/exit

Aperto/Chiuso Open/closed

Arrivi/Partenze Arrivals/departures

Chiuso per restauro Closed for restoration

Chiuso per ferie Closed for holidays

Tirare/Spingere Pull/push

Non toccare Do not touch

Pericolo Danger

Attenzione Beware

Pronto soccorso First aid

Vietato fumare No smoking

ITALIAN

Transport

Traghetto Ferry
Autostazione Bus station
Stazione ferroviaria Train station
Un biglietto a ... A ticket to ...
Solo andata/andata e ritorno One-way/return
A che ora parte? What time does it leave?
Da dove parte? Where does it leave from?

Accommodation

Albergo Hotel
Ha una camera... Do you have a room...
per una/due/tre person(a/e) for one/two/three people
per una/due/tre nott(e/i) for one/two/three nights
con un letto matrimoniale with a double bed
con una doccia/un bagno with a shower/bath
Quanto costa? How much is it?
È compresa la prima colazione? Is breakfast included?
Ha niente che costa di meno Do you have anything cheaper?
La prendo I'll take it
Vorrei prenotare una camera I'd like to book a room
Ho una prenotazione I have a booking
Ostello per la gioventù Youth hostel

In the restaurant

Una tavola A table
Vorrei prenotare I'd like to book
una tavola a table for two
per due alle otto people at eight o'clock
Abbiamo bisogno di un coltello We need a knife
una forchetta a fork
un cucchiaio a spoon
un bicchiere a glass
Che cosa mi consiglia lei? What do you recommend?
Cameriere/a! Waiter/waitress!
Il conto Bill/check
È incluso il servizio? Is service included?
Sono vegetariano/a I'm a vegetarian
Sono vegano/a I'm a vegan
Ho un'allergia a... I have an allergy to...

Questions and directions

Dove? Where?
(Dov'è/Dove sono)? (where is/are ...?)
Quando? When?
Cosa? (Cos'è?) What? (what is it?)
Quanto/Quanti? How much/many?
Perché? Why?
È/C'è È/C'è ...?) It is/there is (is it/is there...?)
Che ora è/Che ore sono What time is it?
Come arrivo a...? How do I get to...?
A che ora apre? What time does it open?
A che ora chiude? What time does it close?
Quanto costa? (Quanto costano?) How much does it cost ? (...do they cost?)
Come si chiama in italiano? What's it called in Italian?

Menu reader

Basics and snacks

Aceto Vinegar
Aglio Garlic
Biscotti Biscuits
Burro Butter
Caramelle Sweets
Cioccolato Chocolate
Focaccia Oven-baked bread- based snack
Formaggio Cheese
Frittata Omelette
Gelato Ice cream
Grissini Bread sticks
Marmellata Jam
Olio Oil
Olive Olives
Pane Bread
Pane integrale Wholemeal bread
Panino Bread roll
Patatine Crisps
Patatine fritte Chips
Pepe Pepper
Pizzetta Small cheese and tomato pizza
Riso Rice
Sale Salt
Tramezzini Sandwich
Uova Eggs
Yogurt Yoghurt
Zucchero Sugar
Zuppa Soup

Starters (Antipasti)

Antipasto misto Mixed cold meats and cheese (and a selection of other things in this list)

Caponata Mixed aubergine, olives, tomatoes and celery

Caprese Tomato and mozzarella salad

Crostini di milza Minced spleen on pieces of toast

Donzele/donzelline Fried dough balls

Fettuna/bruschetta Garlic toast with olive oil

Finocchiona Pork sausage flavoured with fennel

Insalata di mare Seafood salad

Insalata di riso Rice salad

Melanzane in parmigiana Fried aubergine in tomato and parmesan cheese sauce

Mortadella Salami-type cured meat

Pancetta Bacon

Peperonata Grilled green, red or yellow peppers stewed in olive oil

Pinzimonio Raw seasonal vegetables in olive oil, with salt and pepper

Pomodori ripieni Stuffed tomatoes

Prosciutto Ham

Prosciutto di cinghiale Cured wild boar ham

Salame Salami

Salame toscano Pork sausage with pepper and cubes of fat

Salsicce Pork or wild boar sausage

The first course (Il primo)

Soups

Acquacotta Onion soup served with toast and poached egg

Brodo Clear broth

Cacciucco Fish stew with tomatoes, bread and red wine

Carabaccia Onion soup

Garmugia Soup made with fava beans, peas, artichokes, asparagus and bacon

Minestra di farro Wheat and bean soup

Minestrina Any light soup

Minestrone Thick vegetable soup

Minestrone alla fiorentina Haricot bean soup with red cabbage, tomatoes, onions and herbs

Panzanella Summer salad of tomatoes, basil, cucumber, onion and bread

Pappa al pomodoro Tomato soup thickened with bread

Pasta e fagioli Pasta soup with beans

Pastina in brodo Pasta pieces in clear broth

Ribollita Winter vegetable soup, based on beans and thickened with bread

Stracciatella Broth with egg

Zuppa di fagioli Bean soup

Pasta and gnocchi

Cannelloni Large tubes of pasta, stuffed

Farfalle Literally "bow"- shaped pasta; the word also means "butterflies"

Fettuccine Narrow pasta ribbons

Gnocchi Small potato and dough dumplings

Gnocchi di ricotta Dumplings filled with ricotta and spinach

Lasagne Lasagne

Maccheroni Tubular spaghetti

Pappardelle (con lepre) Wide, short noodles, often served with hare sauce

Pasta al forno Pasta baked with minced meat, eggs, tomato and cheese

Pasta alla carrettiera Pasta with tomato, garlic, pepper, parsley and chilli

Penne Smaller version of rigatoni

Penne strasciate Quill-shaped pasta in meat sauce

Ravioli Small packets of stuffed pasta

Rigatoni Large, grooved, tubular pasta

Risotto Cooked rice dish, with sauce

Spaghetti Spaghetti

Spaghettini Thin spaghetti

Tagliatelle Pasta ribbons; another word for fettucine

Tortellini Small rings of pasta, stuffed with meat or cheese

Vermicelli Very thin spaghetti (literally "little worms")

Pasta sauces

Aglio e olio (e peperoncino) Tossed in garlic and olive oil (and hot chillies)

Arrabiata Spicy tomato sauce

Bolognese Meat sauce

Burro e salvia Butter and sage

Carbonara Cream, ham and beaten egg

Frutta di mare Seafood

Funghi Mushroom

Matriciana Cubed pork and tomato sauce
Panna Cream
Parmigiano Parmesan cheese
Pesto Ground basil, pine nut, garlic and pecorino sauce
Pomodoro Tomato sauce
Ragù Meat sauce
Vongole Clam and tomato sauce

The second course (Il secondo)

Meat (carne)

Agnello Lamb
Arista Roast pork loin with garlic and rosemary
Bistecca Steak
Bistecca alla fiorentina Thick grilled T-bone steak
Cibreo Chicken liver and egg stew
Coniglio Rabbit
Costolette Chops
Cotolette Cutlets
Fegatini Chicken livers
Fegato Liver
Involtini Steak slices, rolled and stuffed
Lingua Tongue
Lombatina Veal chop
Maiale Pork
Manzo Beef
Ossobuco Shin of veal
Peposo Peppered beef stew
Pollo Chicken
Pollo alla diavola/ al mattone Chicken flattened with a brick, grilled with herbs
Polpette Meatballs (or minced balls of anything)
Rognoni Kidneys
Salsiccia Sausage
Saltimbocca Veal with ham
Scottiglia Stew of veal, game and poultry, cooked with white wine and tomatoes
Spezzatino Stew
Spiedini di maiale Skewered spiced cubes of pork loin and liver, with bread and bay leaves
Tacchino Turkey
Trippa Tripe
Trippa alla fiorentina Tripe in tomato sauce, served with parmesan
Vitello Veal

Fish (pesce) and shellfish (crostacei)

Acciughe Anchovies
Anguilla Eel
Aragosta Lobster
Baccalà alla livornese Salt cod with garlic, tomatoes and parsley
Bronzino/Branzino Sea bass
Calamari Squid
Caparossoli Shrimps
Cape sante Scallops
Coda di rospo Monkfish
Cozze Mussels
Dentice Dentex (like sea bass)
Gamberetti Shrimps
Gamberi Prawns
Granchio Crab
Orata Bream
Ostriche Oysters
Pescespada Swordfish
Polpo Octopus
Rombo Turbot
San Pietro John Dory
Sarde Sardines
Schie Shrimps
Seppie Cuttlefish
Sogliola Sole
Tonno Tuna
Tonno con fagioli Tuna with white beans and raw onion
Triglie Red mullet
Trota Trout
Vongole Clams

Vegetables (contorni) and salad (insalata)

Asparagi Asparagus
Asparagi alla fiorentina Asparagus with butter, fried egg and cheese
Basilico Basil
Broccoli Broccoli
Capperi Capers
Carciofi Artichokes
Carciofini Artichoke hearts
Carotte Carrots
Cavolfiori Cauliflower
Cavolo Cabbage
Ceci Chickpeas
Cetriolo Cucumber
Cipolla Onion

Fagioli Beans
Fagioli all'uccelletto White beans cooked with tomatoes, garlic and sage
Fagiolini Green beans
Finocchio Fennel
Frittata di carciofi Fried artichoke flan
Funghi Mushrooms
Insalata verde/insalata mista Green salad/mixed salad
Melanzana Aubergine/eggplant
Patate Potatoes
Peperoni Peppers
Piselli Peas
Pomodori Tomatoes
Radicchio Chicory
Spinaci Spinach
Zucca Pumpkin
Zucchini Courgettes

Desserts (dolci)

Amaretti Macaroons
Brigidini Anise wafer biscuits
Buccellato Anise raisin cake
Cantucci/cantuccini Small almond biscuits, served with Vinsanto wine
Cassata Ice cream cake with candied fruit
Castagnaccio Unleavened chestnut-flour cake containing raisins, walnuts and rosemary
Cenci Fried dough dusted with powdered sugar
Frittelle di riso Rice fritters
Gelato Ice cream
Macedonia Fruit salad
Meringa Frozen meringue with whipped cream and chocolate
Necci Chestnut-flour crêpes
Panforte Hard fruit, nut and spice cake
Ricciarelli Marzipan almond biscuits
Schiacciata alla fiorentina Orange-flavoured cake covered with powdered sugar, eaten at carnival time
Schiacciata con l'uva Grape- and sugar-covered bread dessert
Torta Cake, tart
Zabaglione Dessert made with eggs, sugar and Marsala wine
Zuccotto Sponge cake filled with chocolate and whipped cream
Zuppa Inglese Trifle

Cheese (formaggi)

Caciocavallo A type of dried, mature mozzarella cheese
Fontina Northern Italian cheese used in cooking
Gorgonzola Soft blue-veined cheese
Mozzarella Bland, soft white cheese used on pizzas
Parmigiano Parmesan
Pecorino Strong-tasting hard sheep's cheese
Provolone Hard strong cheese
Ricotta Soft white cheese made from ewe's milk, used in sweet or savoury dishes

Fruit and nuts (frutta and noce)

Ananas Pineapple
Arance Oranges
Banane Bananas
Ciliegie Cherries
Fichi Figs
Fragole Strawberries
Limone Lemon
Mandorle Almonds
Mele Apples
Melone Melon
Pere Pears
Pesche Peaches
Pinoli Pine nuts
Pistacchio Pistachio nut
Uve Grapes

Cooking terms

Affumicato Smoked
Al dente Firm, not overcooked
Al ferro Grilled without oil
Al forno Baked
Al Marsala Cooked with Marsala wine
Al vapore Steamed
Alla brace Barbecued
Alla griglia Grilled
Allo spiedo On the spit
Arrosto Roasted
Ben cotto Well done
Bollito Boiled
Brasato Cooked in wine
Cotto Cooked (not raw)
Crudo Raw
Fritto Fried
In umido Stewed

Lesso Boiled
Milanese Fried in egg and breadcrumbs
Pizzaiola Cooked with tomato sauce
Ripieno Stuffed
Sangue Rare
Surgelato Frozen

Drinks

Acqua minerale Mineral water
Alla spina Draught (beer)
Aranciata Orangeade
Bicchiere Glass
Birra Beer
Bottiglia Bottle
Caffè Coffee
Cioccolata calda Hot chocolate
Ghiaccio Ice
Granita Iced coffee or fruit drink

Latte Milk
Limonata Lemonade
Selz Soda water
Spremuta Fresh fruit juice
Spumante Sparkling wine
Succo Concentrated fruit juice with sugar
Tè Tea
Tonico Tonic water
Vino Wine
Rosso Red
Bianco White
Rosato Rosé
Secco Dry
Dolce Sweet
Litro Litre
Mezzo Half
Quarto Quarter
Salute! Cheers!

SMALL PRINT

Publishing information
Fifth edition 2024

Distribution
UK, Ireland and Europe
Apa Publications (UK) Ltd; sales@roughguides.com
United States and Canada
Ingram Publisher Services; ips@ingramcontent.com
Australia and New Zealand
Booktopia; retailer@booktopia.com.au
Worldwide
Apa Publications (UK) Ltd; sales@roughguides.com

Special Sales, Content Licensing and CoPublishing
Rough Guides can be purchased in bulk quantities at discounted prices. We can create special editions, personalised jackets and corporate imprints tailored to your needs. sales@roughguides.com.
roughguides.com

Printed in Czech Republic

This book was produced using **Typefi** automated publishing software.

All rights reserved
© 2024 Apa Digital AG
License edition © Apa Publications Ltd UK

No part of this publication may be reproduced, stored in or introduced into a retrieval system, or transmitted in any form, or by any means (electronic, mechanical, photocopying, recording or otherwise) without the prior written permission of the copyright owner.

A catalogue record for this book is available from the British Library.

The publishers and authors have done their best to ensure the accuracy and currency of all the information in **Pocket Rough Guide Florence**, however, they can accept no responsibility for any loss, injury, or inconvenience sustained by any traveller as a result of information or advice contained in the guide.

Rough Guide credits
Project editor: Joanna Reeves
Copy editor: Tim Binks
Updater: Annie Warren
Cartography: Katie Bennett
Picture editor: Piotr Kala
Picture manager: Tom Smyth
Layout: Pradeep Thapliyal
Original design: Richard Czapnik
Head of DTP and Pre-Press: Rebeka Davies
Head of Publishing: Sarah Clark

About the author

Annie Warren is an editor, writer and translator based in the Midlands. After studying French and Italian at university, she lived in France, Italy and Austria. She loves wild swimming, film photography and strong margaritas. You can follow her @notanniewarren and find more of her work on her website ⓦ annie-warren.com. Annie is a former Rough Guides editor whose portfolio of work includes updating the *Pocket Rough Guide to Rome* and the *Insight Guide to Tuscany*. She builds upon the work of Jonathan Buckley, who has contributed to various Rough Guides and published ten novels; he was also the winner of the 2015 BBC National Short Story Award.

Help us update

We've gone to a lot of effort to ensure that this edition of the **Pocket Rough Guide Florence** is accurate and up-to-date. However, things change – places get "discovered", opening hours are notoriously fickle, restaurants and rooms raise prices or lower standards. If you feel we've got it wrong or left something out, we'd like to know, and if you can remember the address, the price, the hours, the phone number, so much the better.

Please send your comments with the subject line "**Pocket Rough Guide Florence Update**" to mail@uk.roughguides.com. We'll credit all contributions and send a copy of the next edition (or any other Rough Guide if you prefer) for the very best emails.

Photo Credits

(Key: T-top; C-centre; B-bottom; L-left; R-right)

Borgo Antico 108
Antonio Quattrone/Museo dell'Opera del Duomo Firenze 32
Claudio Giovannini/Museo dell'Opera del Duomo Firenze 31
Dario Lasagni/Museo Marino Marini 23T
Diana Jarvis/Rough Guides 2C, 12/13B, 18T, 18B, 19T, 19B, 20T, 21B, 23B, 26, 35, 42, 49, 50, 53, 62, 64, 67, 74, 78, 80, 88, 89, 90, 98, 100, 103, 104
Dorling Kindersley 20C
Dreamstime 2BR
Helena Smith/Rough Guides 24/25
iStock 11T, 12/13T, 13C, 15T, 17T, 18C, 22T, 33, 117, 128/129

James McConnachie/Rough Guides 11B, 20B, 58, 61, 63, 76
Michelle Grant/Rough Guides 16T, 22B, 70, 73, 91
Palazzo Guadagni 118/119
Quattro Leoni 109
Shutterstock 1, 2T, 2BL, 4, 6, 10, 12B, 14B, 14T, 15B, 16B, 17B, 19C, 21T, 21C, 22C, 23C, 34, 37, 41, 45, 56, 59, 77, 81, 86, 93, 94, 97, 101, 102, 106, 111, 112, 113, 114, 116

Cover: View from the Duomo
Shutterstock
Cover flap: All images **Shutterstock**

Index

INDEX

INDEX

NOTES